A DEAL IN WHEAT

COMPLETE
WORKS OF
FRANK
NORRIS

CONTENTS

LIST OF ILLUSTRATIONS

A DEAL IN WHEAT

A DEAL IN WHEAT

I

THE BEAR—WHEAT AT SIXTY-TWO

A S Sam Lewiston backed the horse into the shafts of his buckboard and began hitching the tugs to the whiffletree, his wife came out from the kitchen door of the house and drew near, and stood for some time at the horse's head, her arms folded and her apron rolled around them. For a long moment neither spoke. They had talked over the situation so long and so comprehensively the night before that there seemed to be nothing more to say.

The time was late in the summer, the place a ranch in southwestern Kansas, and Lewiston and his wife were two of a vast population of farmers, wheat growers, who at that moment were passing through a crisis—a crisis that at any moment might culminate in tragedy. Wheat was down to sixty-six.

At length Emma Lewiston spoke.

"Well," she hazarded, looking vaguely out

across the ranch toward the horizon, leagues distant; "well, Sam, there's always that offer of brother Joe's. We can quit—and go to Chicago—if the worst comes."

"And give up!" exclaimed Lewiston, running the lines through the torets. "Leave the ranch! Give up! After all these years!"

His wife made no reply for the moment. Lewiston climbed into the buckboard and gathered up the lines. "Well, here goes for the last try, Emmie," he said. "Good-by, girl. Maybe things will look better in town to-day."

"Maybe," she said gravely. She kissed her husband good-by and stood for some time looking after the buckboard traveling toward the town in a moving pillar of dust.

"I don't know," she murmured at length; "I don't know just how we're going to make out."

When he reached town, Lewiston tied the horse to the iron railing in front of the Odd Fellows' Hall, the ground floor of which was occupied by the post-office, and went across the street and up the stairway of a building of brick and granite—quite the most pretentious structure of the town—and knocked at a door upon the first landing. The door was furnished with a pane of frosted glass, on which, in gold letters, was inscribed, "Bridges & Co., Grain Dealers."

Bridges himself, a middle-aged man who wore a velvet skull-cap and who was smoking a Pittsburg stogie, met the farmer at the counter and the two exchanged perfunctory greetings.

"Well," said Lewiston, tentatively, after awhile.

"Well, Lewiston," said the other, "I can't take that wheat of yours at any better than sixty-two."

"Sixty-*two*."

"It's the Chicago price that does it, Lewiston. Truslow is bearing the stuff for all he's worth. It's Truslow and the bear clique that stick the knife into us. The price broke again this morning. We've just got a wire."

"Good heavens," murmured Lewiston, looking vaguely from side to side. "That—that ruins me. I *can't* carry my grain any longer—what with storage charges and—and—— Bridges, I don't see just how I'm going to make out. Sixty-two cents a bushel! Why, man, what with this and with that it's cost me nearly a dollar a bushel to raise that wheat, and now Truslow——"

He turned away abruptly with a quick gesture of infinite discouragement.

He went down the stairs, and making his

way to where his buckboard was hitched, got in, and, with eyes vacant, the reins slipping and sliding in his limp, half-open hands, drove slowly back to the ranch. His wife had seen him coming, and met him as he drew up before the barn.

"Well?" she demanded.

"Emmie," he said as he got out of the buck-board, laying his arm across her shoulder, "Emmie, I guess we'll take up with Joe's offer. We'll go to Chicago. We're cleaned out!"

II

THE BULL—WHEAT AT A DOLLAR-TEN

. . . —— *and said Party of the Second
Part further covenants and agrees to merchandise
such wheat in foreign ports, it being understood
and agreed between the Party of the First Part
and the Party of the Second Part that the wheat
hereinbefore mentioned is released and sold to the
Party of the Second Part for export purposes only,
and not for consumption or distribution within
the boundaries of the United States of America
or of Canada.*

"Now, Mr. Gates, if you will sign for Mr.
Truslow I guess that'll be all," remarked
Hornung when he had finished reading.

Hornung affixed his signature to the two
documents and passed them over to Gates,
who signed for his principal and client, Truslow
—or, as he had been called ever since he had
gone into the fight against Hornung's corner—
the Great Bear. Hornung's secretary was
called in and witnessed the signatures, and
Gates thrust the contract into his Gladstone
bag and stood up, smoothing his hat.

7

"You will deliver the warehouse receipts for the grain," began Gates.

"I'll send a messenger to Truslow's office before noon," interrupted Hornung. "You can pay by certified check through the Illinois Trust people."

When the other had taken himself off, Hornung sat for some moments gazing abstractedly toward his office windows, thinking over the whole matter. He had just agreed to release to Truslow, at the rate of one dollar and ten cents per bushel, one hundred thousand out of the two million and odd bushels of wheat that he, Hornung, controlled, or actually owned. And for the moment he was wondering if, after all, he had done wisely in not goring the Great Bear to actual financial death. He had made him pay one hundred thousand dollars. Truslow was good for this amount. Would it not have been better to have put a prohibitive figure on the grain and forced the Bear into bankruptcy? True, Hornung would then be without his enemy's money, but Truslow would have been eliminated from the situation, and that—so Hornung told himself—was always a consummation most devoutly, strenuously and diligently to be striven for. Truslow once dead was dead, but the Bear was never more dangerous than when desperate.

"But so long as he can't get *wheat*," muttered Hornung at the end of his reflections, "he can't hurt me.   And he can't get it.   That I *know*."

For Hornung controlled the situation.   So far back as the February of that year an "unknown bull" had been making his presence felt on the floor of the Board of Trade.   By the middle of March the commercial reports of the daily press had begun to speak of "the powerful bull clique"; a few weeks later that legendary condition of affairs implied and epitomized in the magic words "Dollar Wheat" had been attained, and by the first of April, when the price had been boosted to one dollar and ten cents a bushel, Hornung had disclosed his hand, and in place of mere rumours, the definite and authoritative news that May wheat had been cornered in the Chicago pit went flashing around the world from Liverpool to Odessa and from Duluth to Buenos Ayres.

It was—so the veteran operators were persuaded—Truslow himself who had made Hornung's corner possible.   The Great Bear had for once over-reached himself, and, believing himself all-powerful, had hammered the price just the fatal fraction too far down. Wheat had gone to sixty-two—for the time, and under the circumstances, an abnormal price.

When the reaction came it was tremendous. Hornung saw his chance, seized it, and in a few months had turned the tables, had cornered the product, and virtually driven the bear clique out of the pit.

On the same day that the delivery of the hundred thousand bushels was made to Truslow, Hornung met his broker at his lunch club.

"Well," said the latter, "I see you let go that line of stuff to Truslow."

Hornung nodded; but the broker added:

"Remember, I was against it from the very beginning. I know we've cleared up over a hundred thou'. I would have fifty times preferred to have lost twice that and *smashed Truslow dead*. Bet you what you like he makes us pay for it somehow."

"Huh!" grunted his principal. "How about insurance, and warehouse charges, and carrying expenses on that lot? Guess we'd have had to pay those, too, if we'd held on."

But the other put up his chin, unwilling to be persuaded. "I won't sleep easy," he declared, "till Truslow is busted."

III

JUST as Going mounted the steps on the edge of the pit the great gong struck, a roar of a hundred voices developed with the swiftness of successive explosions, the rush of a hundred men surging downward to the centre of the pit filled the air with the stamp and grind of feet, a hundred hands in eager strenuous gestures tossed upward from out the brown of the crowd, the official reporter in his cage on the margin of the pit leaned far forward with straining ear to catch the opening bid, and another day of battle was begun.

Since the sale of the hundred thousand bushels of wheat to Truslow the "Hornung crowd" had steadily shouldered the price higher until on this particular morning it stood at one dollar and a half. That was Hornung's price. No one else had any grain to sell.

But not ten minutes after the opening, Going was surprised out of all countenance to hear shouted from the other side of the pit these words:

"Sell May at one-fifty."

Going was for the moment touching elbows with Kimbark on one side and with Merriam on the other, all three belonging to the "Hornung crowd." Their answering challenge of "*Sold*" was as the voice of one man. They did not pause to reflect upon the strangeness of the circumstance. (That was for afterward.) Their response to the offer was as unconscious as reflex action and almost as rapid, and before the pit was well aware of what had happened the transaction of one thousand bushels was down upon Going's trading-card and fifteen hundred dollars had changed hands. But here was a marvel—the whole available supply of wheat cornered, Hornung master of the situation, invincible, unassailable; yet behold a man willing to sell, a Bear bold enough to raise his head.

"That was Kennedy, wasn't it, who made that offer?" asked Kimbark, as Going noted down the trade—"Kennedy, that new man?"

"Yes; who do you suppose he's selling for; who's willing to go short at this stage of the game?"

"Maybe he ain't short."

"Short! Great heavens, man; where'd he get the stuff?"

"Blamed if I know. We can account for

every handful of May. Steady! Oh, there he goes again."

"Sell a thousand May at one-fifty," vociferated the bear-broker, throwing out his hand, one finger raised to indicate the number of "contracts" offered. This time it was evident that he was attacking the Hornung crowd deliberately, for, ignoring the jam of traders that swept toward him, he looked across the pit to where Going and Kimbark were shouting "*Sold! Sold!*" and nodded his head.

A second time Going made memoranda of the trade, and either the Hornung holdings were increased by two thousand bushels of May wheat or the Hornung bank account swelled by at least three thousand dollars of some unknown short's money.

Of late—so sure was the bull crowd of its position—no one had even thought of glancing at the inspection sheet on the bulletin board. But now one of Going's messengers hurried up to him with the announcement that this sheet showed receipts at Chicago for that morning of twenty-five thousand bushels, and not credited to Hornung. Some one had got hold of a line of wheat overlooked by the "clique" and was dumping it upon them.

"Wire the Chief," said Going over his shoulder to Merriam. This one struggled out of the crowd, and on a telegraph blank scribbled:

"Strong bear movement—New man—Kennedy—Selling in lots of five contracts—Chicago receipts twenty-five thousand."

The message was despatched, and in a few moments the answer came back, laconic, of military terseness:

"Support the market."

And Going obeyed, Merriam and Kimbark following, the new broker fairly throwing the wheat at them in thousand-bushel lots.

"Sell May at 'fifty; sell May; sell May." A moment's indecision, an instant's hesitation, the first faint suggestion of weakness, and the market would have broken under them. But for the better part of four hours they stood their ground, taking all that was offered, in constant communication with the Chief, and from time to time stimulated and steadied by his brief, unvarying command:

"Support the market."

At the close of the session they had bought in the twenty-five thousand bushels of May. Hornung's position was as stable as a rock, and the price closed even with the opening figure—one dollar and a half.

But the morning's work was the talk of all La Salle Street. Who was back of the raid?

What was the meaning of this unexpected selling? For weeks the pit trading had been merely nominal. Truslow, the Great Bear, from whom the most serious attack might have been expected, had gone to his country seat at Geneva Lake, in Wisconsin, declaring himself to be out of the market entirely. He went bass-fishing every day.

IV

ON a certain day toward the middle of the month, at a time when the mysterious Bear had unloaded some eighty thousand bushels upon Hornung, a conference was held in the library of Hornung's home. His broker attended it, and also a clean-faced, bright-eyed individual whose name of Cyrus Ryder might have been found upon the pay-roll of a rather well-known detective agency. For upward of half an hour after the conference began the detective spoke, the other two listening attentively, gravely.

"Then, last of all," concluded Ryder, "I made out I was a hobo, and began stealing rides on the Belt Line Railroad. Know the road? It just circles Chicago. Truslow owns it. Yes? Well, then I began to catch on. I noticed that cars of certain numbers—thirty-one nought thirty-four, thirty-two one ninety— well, the numbers don't matter, but anyhow, these cars were always switched onto the sidings by Mr. Truslow's main elevator D soon as they came in. The wheat was shunted in, and they were pulled out again. Well, I spotted one car and stole a ride on her. Say, look here, *that car went right around the city on the Belt, and came back to D again, and the same wheat in her all the time.* The grain was re-inspected—it was raw, I tell you—and the warehouse receipts made out just as though the stuff had come in from Kansas or Iowa."

"The same wheat all the time!" interrupted Hornung.

"The same wheat—your wheat, that you sold to Truslow."

"Great snakes!" ejaculated Hornung's broker. "Truslow never took it abroad at all."

"Took it abroad! Say, he's just been running it around Chicago, like the supers in 'Shenandoah,' round an' round, so you'd think it was a new lot, an' selling it back to you again."

"No wonder we couldn't account for so much wheat."

"Bought it from us at one-ten, and made us buy it back—our own wheat—at one-fifty."

Hornung and his broker looked at each other in silence for a moment. Then all at once Hornung struck the arm of his chair with his fist and exploded in a roar of laughter. The broker stared for one bewildered moment, then followed his example.

"Sold! Sold!" shouted Hornung almost gleefully. "Upon my soul it's as good as a Gilbert and Sullivan show. And we—— Oh, Lord! Billy, shake on it, and hats off to my distinguished friend, Truslow. He'll be President some day. Hey! What? Prosecute him? Not I."

"He's done us out of a neat hatful of dollars for all that," observed the broker, suddenly grave.

"Billy, it's worth the price."

"We've got to make it up somehow."

"Well, tell you what. We were going to boost the price to one seventy-five next week, and make that our settlement figure."

"Can't do it now. Can't afford it."

"No. Here; we'll let out a big link; we'll put wheat at two dollars, and let it go at that."

"Two it is, then," said the broker.

V

THE BREAD LINE

THE street was very dark and absolutely deserted. It was a district on the "South Side," not far from the Chicago River, given up largely to wholesale stores, and after nightfall was empty of all life. The echoes slept but lightly hereabouts, and the slightest footfall, the faintest noise, woke them upon the instant and sent them clamouring up and down the length of the pavement between the iron shuttered fronts. The only light visible came from the side door of a certain "Vienna" bakery, where at one o'clock in the morning loaves of bread were given away to any who should ask. Every evening about nine o'clock the outcasts began to gather about the side door. The stragglers came in rapidly, and the line—the "bread line," as it was called—began to form. By midnight it was usually some hundred yards in length, stretching almost the entire length of the block.

Toward ten in the evening, his coat collar turned up against the fine drizzle that pervaded the air, his hands in his pockets, his elbows gripping his sides, Sam Lewiston came up and silently took his place at the end of the line.

Unable to conduct his farm upon a paying basis at the time when Truslow, the "Great Bear," had sent the price of grain down to sixty-two cents a bushel, Lewiston had turned over his entire property to his creditors, and, leaving Kansas for good, had abandoned farming, and had left his wife at her sister's boarding-house in Topeka with the understanding that she was to join him in Chicago so soon as he had found a steady job. Then he had come to Chicago and had turned workman. His brother Joe conducted a small hat factory on Archer Avenue, and for a time he found there a meager employment. But difficulties had occurred, times were bad, the hat factory was involved in debts, the repealing of a certain import duty on manufactured felt overcrowded the home market with cheap Belgian and French products, and in the end his brother had assigned and gone to Milwaukee.

Thrown out of work, Lewiston drifted aimlessly about Chicago, from pillar to post, working a little, earning here a dollar, there a dime, but always sinking, sinking, till at last the ooze of the lowest bottom dragged at his feet and the rush of the great ebb went over him and engulfed him and shut him out from the light, and a park bench became his home and the "bread line" his chief makeshift of subsistence.

He stood now in the enfolding drizzle, sodden, stupefied with fatigue. Before and behind stretched the line. There was no talking. There was no sound. The street was empty. It was so still that the passing of a cable-car in the adjoining thoroughfare grated like prolonged rolling explosions, beginning and ending at immeasurable distances. The drizzle descended incessantly. After a long time midnight struck.

There was something ominous and gravely impressive in this interminable line of dark figures, close-pressed, soundless; a crowd, yet absolutely still; a close-packed, silent file, waiting, waiting in the vast deserted night-ridden street; waiting without a word, without a movement, there under the night and under the slow-moving mists of rain.

Few in the crowd were professional beggars. Most of them were workmen, long since out of work, forced into idleness by long-continued "hard times," by ill luck, by sickness. To them the "bread line" was a godsend. At least they could not starve. Between jobs here in the end was something to hold them up —a small platform, as it were, above the sweep of black water, where for a moment they might pause and take breath before the plunge.

The period of waiting on this night of rain seemed endless to those silent, hungry men; but at length there was a stir.   The line moved. The side door opened.   Ah, at last!   They were going to hand out the bread.

But instead of the usual white-aproned under-cook with his crowded hampers there now appeared in the doorway a new man—a young fellow who looked like a bookkeeper's assistant. He bore in his hand a placard, which he tacked to the outside of the door.   Then he disap-peared within the bakery, locking the door after him.

A shudder of poignant despair, an unformed, inarticulate sense of calamity, seemed to run from end to end of the line.   What had hap-pened?   Those in the rear, unable to read the placard, surged forward, a sense of bitter dis-appointment clutching at their hearts.

The line broke up, disintegrated into a shape-less throng—a throng that crowded forward and collected in front of the shut door whereon the placard was affixed.   Lewiston, with the others, pushed forward.   On the placard he read these words:

"Owing to the fact that the price of grain has been increased to two dollars a bushel, there will be no distribution of bread from this bakery until further notice."

Lewiston turned away, dumb, bewildered. Till morning he walked the streets, going on without purpose, without direction. But now at last his luck had turned. Overnight the wheel of his fortunes had creaked and swung upon its axis, and before noon he had found a job in the street-cleaning brigade. In the course of time he rose to be first shift-boss, then deputy inspector, then inspector, promoted to the dignity of driving in a red wagon with rubber tires and drawing a salary instead of mere wages. The wife was sent for and a new start made.

But Lewiston never forgot. Dimly he began to see the significance of things. Caught once in the cogs and wheels of a great and terrible engine, he had seen—none better—its workings. Of all the men who had vainly stood in the "bread line" on that rainy night in early summer, he, perhaps, had been the only one who had struggled up to the surface again. How many others had gone down in the great ebb? Grim question; he dared not think how many.

He had seen the two ends of a great wheat operation—a battle between Bear and Bull. The stories (subsequently published in the

city's press) of Truslow's countermove in selling Hornung his own wheat, supplied the
unseen section. The farmer—he who raised
the wheat—was ruined upon one hand; the
working-man—he who consumed it—was ruined
upon the other. But between the two, the
great operators, who never saw the wheat they
traded in, bought and sold the world's food,
gambled in the nourishment of entire nations,
practised their tricks, their chicanery and
oblique shifty "deals," were reconciled in their
differences, and went on through their appointed
way, jovial, contented, enthroned, and unassailable.

THE WIFE OF CHINO

THE WIFE OF CHINO

I

CHINO'S WIFE

ON the back porch of the "office," young
Lockwood—his boots, stained with the
mud of the mines and with candle-drippings,
on the rail—sat smoking his pipe and looking
off down the cañon.

It was early in the evening. Lockwood,
because he had heard the laughter and horse-
play of the men of the night shift as they went
down the cañon from the bunk-house to the
tunnel-mouth, knew that it was a little after
seven. It would not be necessary to go indoors
and begin work on the columns of figures of
his pay-roll for another hour yet. He knocked
the ashes out of his pipe, refilled and lighted it—
stoppering with his match-box—and shot a
wavering blue wreath out over the porch railing. Then he resettled himself in his tilted
chair, hooked his thumbs into his belt, and
fetched a long breath.

For the last few moments he had been con-

29

sidering, in that comfortable spirit of relaxed attention that comes with the after-dinner tobacco, two subjects: first, the beauty of the evening; second, the temperament, character, and appearance of Felice Zavalla.

As for the evening, there could be no two opinions about that. It was charming. The Hand-over-fist Gravel Mine, though not in the higher Sierras, was sufficiently above the level of the mere foot-hills to be in the sphere of influence of the greater mountains. Also, it was remote, difficult of access. Iowa Hill, the nearest post-office, was a good eight miles distant, by trail, across the Indian River. It was sixteen miles by stage from Iowa Hill to Colfax, on the line of the Overland Railroad, and all of a hundred miles from Colfax to San Francisco.

To Lockwood's mind this isolation was in itself an attraction. Tucked away in this fold of the Sierras, forgotten, remote, the little community of a hundred souls that comprised the *personnel* of the Hand-over-fist lived out its life with the completeness of an independent State, having its own government, its own institutions and customs. Besides all this, it had its own dramas as well—little complications that developed with the swiftness of whirl-pools, and that trended toward culmination

with true Western directness. Lockwood,
college-bred—he was a graduate of the Columbia School of Mines—found the life interesting.
On this particular evening he sat over his
pipe rather longer than usual, seduced by the
beauty of the scene and the moment. It was
very quiet. The prolonged rumble of the
mine's stamp-mill came to his ears in a ceaseless
diapason, but the sound was so much a matter
of course that Lockwood no longer heard it.
The millions of pines and redwoods that
covered the flanks of the mountains were
absolutely still. No wind was stirring in their
needles. But the chorus of tree-toads, dry,
staccato, was as incessant as the pounding
of the mill. Far-off—thousands of miles, it
seemed—an owl was hooting, three velvet-soft
notes at exact intervals. A cow in the stable
near at hand lay down with a long breath,
while from the back veranda of Chino Zavalla's
cabin came the clear voice of Felice singing
"The Spanish Cavalier" while she washed the
dishes.
The twilight was fading; the glory that had
blazed in cloudless vermilion and gold over
the divide was dying down like receding music.
The mountains were purple-black. From the
cañon rose the night mist, pale blue, while
above it stood the smoke from the mill, a

motionless plume of sable, shot through by the
last ruddiness of the afterglow.

The air was full of pleasant odours—the
smell of wood fires from the cabins of the
married men and from the ovens of the cook-
house, the ammoniacal whiffs from the stables,
the smell of ripening apples from "Boston's"
orchard—while over all and through all came
the perfume of the witch-hazel and tar-weed
from the forests and mountain sides, as pun-
gent as myrrh, as aromatic as aloes.

> "And if I should fall,
> In vain I would call,"

sang Felice.

Lockwood took his pipe from his teeth and
put back his head to listen. Felice had as good
a voice as so pretty a young woman should
have had. She was twenty-two or twenty-
three years of age, and was incontestably the
beauty of the camp. She was Mexican-
Spanish, tall and very slender, black-haired, as
lithe as a cat, with a cat's green eyes and with
all of a cat's purring, ingratiating insinuation.

Lockwood could not have told exactly just
how the first familiarity between him and
Felice had arisen. It had grown by almost
imperceptible degrees up to a certain point;
now it was a chance meeting on the trail
between the office and the mill, now a frag-

ment of conversation apropos of a letter to be mailed, now a question as to some regulation of the camp, now a detail of repairs done to the cabin wherein Felice lived. As said above, up to a certain point the process of "getting acquainted" had been gradual, and on Lockwood's part unconscious; but beyond that point affairs had progressed rapidly.

At first Felice had been, for Lockwood, a pretty woman, neither more nor less; but by degrees she emerged from this vague classification: she became a very pretty woman. Then she became a personality; she occupied a place within the circle which Lockwood called his world, his life. For the past months this place had, perforce, to be enlarged. Lockwood allowed it to expand. To make room for Felice, he thrust aside, or allowed the idea of Felice to thrust aside, other objects which long had sat secure. The invasion of the woman into the sphere of his existence developed at the end into a thing veritably headlong. Deep-seated convictions, old-established beliefs and ideals, even the two landmarks right and wrong, were hustled and shouldered about as the invasion widened and penetrated. This state of affairs was further complicated by the fact that Felice was the wife of Chino Zavalla, shift-boss of No. 4 gang in the new workings.

II

It was quite possible that, though Lockwood could not have told when and how the acquaintance between him and Felice began and progressed, the young woman herself could. But this is guesswork. Felice being a woman, and part Spanish at that, was vastly more self-conscious, more disingenuous, than the man, the Anglo-Saxon. Also she had that fearlessness that very pretty women have. In her more refined and city-bred sisters this fearlessness would be called poise, or, at the most, "cheek."

And she was quite capable of making young Lockwood, the superintendent, her employer, and nominally the ruler of her little world, fall in love with her. It is only fair to Felice to say that she would not do this deliberately. She would be more conscious of the business than the man, than Lockwood; but in affairs such as this, involving women like Felice, there is a distinction between deliberately doing a thing and consciously doing it.

35

Admittedly this is complicated, but it must be understood that Felice herself was complex, and she could no more help attracting men to her than the magnet the steel filings. It made no difference whether the man was the "breed" boy who split logging down by the engine-house or the young superintendent with his college education, his white hands and dominating position; over each and all who came within range of her influence Felice, with her black hair and green eyes, her slim figure and her certain indefinite "cheek"— which must not by any manner of means be considered as "boldness"—cast the weird of her kind.

If one understood her kind, knew how to make allowances, knew just how seriously to take her eyes and her "cheek," no great harm was done. Otherwise, consequences were very apt to follow.

Hicks was one of those who from the very first had understood. Hicks was the manager of the mine, and Lockwood's chief—in a word, *the boss*. He was younger even than Lockwood, a boy virtually, but a wonderful boy—a boy such as only America, western America at that, could produce, masterful, self-controlled, incredibly capable, as taciturn as a sphinx, strong of mind and of muscle, and possessed of a cold gray eye that was as penetrating as chilled steel.

To this person, impersonal as force itself, Felice had once, by some mysterious feminine art, addressed, in all innocence, her little maneuver of fascination. One lift of the steady eyelid, one quiet glint of that terrible cold gray eye, that poniarded her every tissue of complexity, inconsistency, and coquetry, had been enough. Felice had fled the field from this young fellow, so much her junior, and then afterward, in a tremor of discomfiture and distress, had kept her distance.

Hicks understood Felice. Also the great majority of the miners—shift-bosses, chuck-tenders, bed-rock cleaners, and the like—understood. Lockwood did not.

It may appear difficult of belief that the men, the crude, simple workmen, knew how to take Felice Zavalla, while Lockwood, with all his education and superior intelligence, failed in his estimate of her. The explanation lies no doubt in the fact that in these man-and-woman affairs instinct is a surer guide than education and intelligence, unless, indeed, the intelligence is preternaturally keen. Lockwood's student life had benumbed the elemental instinct, which in the miners, the "men," yet remained vigorous and unblunted, and by means of which

they assessed Felice and her harmless blandish-
ments at their true worth. For all Lockwood's
culture, his own chuck-tenders, unlettered
fellows, cumbersome, slow-witted, "knew
women"—at least, women of their own world,
like Felice—better than he. On the other
hand, his intelligence was no such perfected
instrument as Hicks's, as exact as logarithms,
as penetrating as a scalpel, as uncoloured by
emotions as a steel trap.

Lockwood's life had been a narrow one. He
had studied too hard at Columbia to see much
of the outside world, and he had come straight
from his graduation to take his first position.
Since then his life had been spent virtually in
the wilderness, now in Utah, now in Arizona,
now in British Columbia, and now, at last, in
Placer County, California. His lot was the
common lot of young mining engineers. It
might lead one day to great wealth, but mean-
while it was terribly isolated.

Living thus apart from the world, Lockwood
very easily allowed his judgment to get, as it
were, out of perspective. Class distinctions
lost their sharpness, and one woman—as, for
instance, Felice—was very like another—as, for
instance, the girls his sisters knew "back home"
in New York.

As a last result, the passions were strong.

Things were done "for all they were worth" in Placer County, California. When a man worked, he worked hard; when he slept, he slept soundly; when he hated, he hated with primeval intensity; and when he loved he grew reckless.

It was all one that Felice was Chino's wife. Lockwood swore between his teeth that she should be *his* wife. He had arrived at this conclusion on the night that he sat on the back porch of his office and watched the moon coming up over the Hog Back. He stood up at length and thrust his pipe into his pocket, and putting an arm across the porch pillar, leaned his forehead against it and looked out far in the purple shadows.

"It's madness," he muttered; "yet, I know it—sheer madness; but, by the Lord! I *am* mad—and I don't care."

III

CHINO GOES TO TOWN

As time went on the matter became more involved. Hicks was away. Chino Zavalla, stolid, easy-going, came and went about his work on the night shift, always touching his cap to Lockwood when the two crossed each other's paths, always good-natured, always respectful, seeing nothing but his work.

Every evening, when not otherwise engaged, Lockwood threw a saddle over one of the horses and rode in to Iowa Hill for the mail, returning to the mine between ten and eleven. On one of these occasions, as he drew near to Chino's cabin, a slim figure came toward him down the road and paused at his horse's head. Then he was surprised to hear Felice's voice asking, " 'Ave you a letter for me, then, Meester Lockwude?"

Felice made an excuse of asking thus for her mail each night that Lockwood came from town, and for a month they kept up appearances; but after that they dropped even that pretense, and as often as he met her Lockwood

41

dismounted and walked by her side till the
light in the cabin came into view through the
chaparral.

At length Lockwood made a mighty effort.
He knew how very far he had gone beyond the
point where between the two landmarks called
right and wrong a line is drawn.   He contrived
to keep away from Felice.   He sent one of the
men into town for the mail, and he found
reasons to be in the mine itself whole half-days
at a time.   Whenever a moment's leisure
impended, he took his shotgun and tramped
the mine ditch for leagues, looking for quail
and gray squirrels. For three weeks he so
managed that he never once caught sight of
Felice's black hair and green eyes, never once
heard the sound of her singing.

But the madness was upon him none the less,
and it rode and roweled him like a hag from
dawn to dark and from dark to dawn again,
till in his complete loneliness, in the isolation of
that simple, primitive life, where no congenial
mind relieved the monotony by so much as a
word, morbid, hounded, tortured, the man
grew desperate—was ready for anything that
would solve the situation.

Once every two weeks Lockwood "cleaned up
and amalgamated"—that is to say, the mill was
stopped and the "ripples" where the gold was

caught were scraped clean. Then the ore was sifted out, melted down, and poured into the mould, whence it emerged as the "brick," a dun-coloured rectangle, rough-edged, immensely heavy, which represented anywhere from two to six thousand dollars. This was sent down by express to the smelting-house.

But it was necessary to take the brick from the mine to the express office at Iowa Hill.

This duty devolved upon Lockwood and Chino Zavalla. Hicks had from the very first ordered that the Spaniard should accompany the superintendent upon this mission. Zavalla was absolutely trustworthy, as honest as the daylight, strong physically, cool-headed, discreet, and—to Hicks's mind a crowning recommendation—close-mouthed. For about the mine it was never known when the brick went to town or who took it. Hicks had impressed this fact upon Zavalla. He was to tell nobody that he was delegated to this duty. "Not even"—Hicks had leveled a forefinger at Chino, and the cold eyes drove home the injunction as the steam-hammer drives the rivet—"not even your wife." And Zavalla had promised. He would have trifled with dynamite sooner than with one of Hicks's orders.

So the fortnightly trips to town in company with Lockwood were explained in various fashions to Felice. She never knew that the mail-bag strapped to her husband's shoulders on those occasions carried some five thousand dollars' worth of bullion.

On a certain Friday in early June Lockwood had amalgamated, and the brick, duly stamped, lay in the safe in the office. The following night he and Chino, who was relieved from mine duty on these occasions, were to take it in to Iowa Hill.

Late Saturday afternoon, however, the engineer's boy brought word to Chino that the superintendent wanted him at once. Chino found Lockwood lying upon the old lounge in the middle room of the office, his foot in bandages.

"Here's luck, Chino," he exclaimed, as the Mexican paused on the threshold. "Come in and—shut the door," he added in a lower voice.

"*Dios!*" murmured Chino. "An accident?"

"Rather," growled Lockwood. "That fool boy, Davis's kid—the car-boy, you know—ran me down in the mine. I yelled at him. Somehow he couldn't stop. Two wheels went over my foot—and the car loaded, too."

Chino shuddered politely.

"Now here's the point," continued Lockwood. "Um—there's nobody round outside there? Take a look, Chino, by the window there. All clear, eh? Well, here's the point. That brick ought to go in to-night just the same, hey?"

"Oh—of a surety, of a surety." Chino spoke in Spanish.

"Now I don't want to let any one else take my place—you never can tell—the beggars will talk. Not all like you, Chino."

"*Gracias, signor.* It is an honour."

"Do you think you can manage alone? I guess you can, hey? No reason why you couldn't."

Chino shut his eyes tight and put up a palm. "Rest assured of that, Signor Lockwude. Rest assured of that."

"Well, get around here about nine."

"It is understood, signor."

Lockwood, who had a passable knowledge of telegraphy, had wired to the Hill for the doctor. About suppertime one appeared, and Lockwood bore the pain of the setting with such fortitude as he could command. He had his supper served in the office. The doctor shared it with him and kept him company.

During the early hours of the evening Lockwood lay on the sofa trying to forget the pain. There was no easier way of doing this than by thinking of Felice. Inevitably his thoughts reverted to her. Now that he was helpless, he could secure no diversion by plunging into the tunnel, giving up his mind to his work. He could not now take down his gun and tramp the ditch. Now he was supine, and the longing to break through the mesh, wrestle free from the complication, gripped him and racked him with all its old-time force.

Promptly at nine o'clock the faithful Chino presented himself at the office. He had one of the two horses that were used by Lockwood as saddle animals, and as he entered he opened his coat and tapped the hilt of a pistol showing from his trousers pocket, with a wink and a grin. Lockwood took the brick from the safe, strapped it into the mail-bag, and Chino, swinging it across his shoulders, was gone, leaving Lockwood to hop back to the sofa, there to throw himself down and face once more his trouble.

IV

WHAT made it harder for Lockwood just now was that even on that very day, in spite of all precaution, in spite of all good resolutions, he had at last seen Felice. Doubtless the young woman herself had contrived it; but, be that as it may, Lockwood, returning from a tour of inspection along the ditch, came upon her not far from camp, but in a remote corner, and she had of course demanded why he kept away from her. What Lockwood said in response he could not now remember; nor, for that matter, was any part of the conversation very clear to his memory. The reason for this was that, just as he was leaving her, something of more importance than conversation had happened. Felice had looked at him.

And she had so timed her look, had so insinuated it into the little, brief, significant silences between their words, that its meaning had been very clear. Lockwood had left her with his brain dizzy, his teeth set, his feet stumbling

47

and fumbling down the trail, for now he knew that Felice wanted him to know that she regretted the circumstance of her marriage to Chino Zavalla; he knew that she wanted him to know that the situation was as intolerable for her as for him.

All the rest of the day, even at this moment, in fact, this new phase of the affair intruded its pregnant suggestions upon his mind, to the exclusion of everything else. He felt the drift strong around him; he knew that in the end he would resign himself to it. At the same time he sensed the abyss, felt the nearness of some dreadful, nameless cataclysm, a thing of black shadow, bottomless, terrifying.

"Lord!" he murmured, as he drew his hand across his forehead, "Lord! I wonder where this thing is going to fetch up."

As he spoke, the telegraph key on his desk, near at hand, began all at once to click off his call. Groaning and grumbling, Lockwood heaved himself up, and, with his right leg bent, hobbled from chair-back to chair-back over to the desk. He rested his right knee on his desk chair, reached for his key, opened the circuit, and answered. There was an instant's pause, then the instrument began to click again. The message was from the express messenger at Iowa Hill.

Word by word Lockwood took it off as follows:

> *"Reno—Kid—will—attempt—hold-up—of—*
> *brick—on—trail—to-night—do—not—send—*
> *till—advised—at—this—end."*

Lockwood let go the key and jumped back from the desk, lips compressed, eyes alight, his fists clenched till the knuckles grew white. The whole figure of him stiffened as tense as drawn wire, braced rigid like a finely bred hound "making game."

Chino was already half an hour gone by the trail, and the Reno Kid was a desperado of the deadliest breed known to the West. How he came to turn up here there was no time to inquire. He was on hand, that was the point; and Reno Kid always "shot to kill." This would be no mere hold-up; it would be murder.

Just then, as Lockwood snatched open a certain drawer of his desk where he kept his revolver, he heard from down the road, in the direction of Chino's cabin, Felice's voice singing:

> "To the war I must go,
> To fight for my country and you, dear."

Lockwood stopped short, his arm at full stretch, still gripping tight the revolver that he had half pulled from the drawer—stopped short and listened.

The solution of everything had come.

He saw it in a flash. The knife hung poised over the knot—even at that moment was falling. Nothing was asked of him—nothing but inertia.

For an instant, alone there in that isolated mining-camp, high above the world, lost and forgotten in the gloom of the cañons and redwoods, Lockwood heard the crisis of his life come crashing through the air upon him like the onslaught of a whirlwind. For an instant, and no more, he considered. Then he cried aloud:

"No, no; I can't, I *can't*—not this way!" And with the words he threw the belt of the revolver about his hips and limped and scampered from the room, drawing the buckle close.

How he gained the stable he never knew, nor how he backed the horse from the building, nor how, hopping on one leg, he got the headstall on and drew the cinches tight.

But the wrench of pain in his foot as, swinging up at last, he tried to catch his off stirrup was reality enough to clear any confusion of spirit. Hanging on as best he might with his knees and one foot, Lockwood, threshing the horse's flanks with the stinging quirt that tapered from the reins of the bridle, shot from the camp in a swirl of clattering hoofs, flying pebbles and blinding clouds of dust.

V

THE TRAIL

THE night was black dark under the red-woods, so impenetrable that he could not see his horse's head, and braced even as he was for greater perils it required all his courage to ride top-speed at this vast slab of black that like a wall he seemed to charge head down with every leap of his bronco's hoofs.

For the first half-hour the trail mounted steadily, then, by the old gravel-pits, it topped the divide and swung down over more open slopes, covered only with chaparral and second growths. Here it was lighter, and Lockwood uttered a fervent "Thank God!" when, a few moments later, the moon shouldered over the mountain crests ahead of him and melted the black shadows to silver-gray. Beyond the gravel-pits the trail turned and followed the flank of the slope, level here for nearly a mile. Lockwood set his teeth against the agony of his foot and gave the bronco the quirt with all his strength.

In another half-hour he had passed Cold

Cañon, and twenty minutes after that had
begun the descent into Indian River. He
forded the river at a gallop, and, with the water
dripping from his very hat-brim, drove labouring under the farther slope.

Then he drew rein with a cry of bewilderment
and apprehension. The lights of Iowa Hill
were not two hundred yards distant. He had
covered the whole distance from the mine, and
where was Chino?

There was but one answer: back there along
the trail somewhere, at some point by which
Lockwood had galloped headlong and unheed-
ing, lying up there in the chaparral with
Reno's bullets in his body.

There was no time now to go on to the Hill.
Chino, if he was not past help, needed it without
an instant's loss of time. Lockwood spun the
horse about. Once more the ford, once more
the cañon slopes, once more the sharp turn by
Cold Cañon, once more the thick darkness
under the redwoods. Steadily he galloped on,
searching the roadside.

Then all at once he reined in sharply, bringing the horse to a standstill, one ear turned
down the wind. The night's silence was
broken by a multitude of sounds—the laboured
breathing of the spent bronco, the saddle creak-
ing as the dripping flanks rose and fell, the

touch of wind in the tree-tops and the chorusing of the myriad tree-toads. But through all these, distinct, as precise as a clock-tick, Lockwood had heard, and yet distinguished, the click of a horse's hoof drawing near, and the horse was at a gallop: Reno at last.

Lockwood drew his pistol. He stood in thick shadow. Only some twenty yards in front of him was there any faintest break in the darkness; but at that point the blurred moonlight made a grayness across the trail, just a tone less deep than the redwoods' shadows.

With his revolver cocked and trained upon this patch of grayness, Lockwood waited, holding his breath.

The gallop came blundering on, sounding in the night's silence as loud as the passage of an express train; and the echo of it, flung back from the cañon side, confused it and distorted it till, to Lockwood's morbid alertness, it seemed fraught with all the madness of flight, all the hurry of desperation.

Then the hoof-beats rose to a roar, and a shadow just darker than the darkness heaved against the grayness that Lockwood held covered with his pistol. Instantly he shouted aloud:

"Halt! Throw up your hands!"

His answer was a pistol shot.

He dug his heels to his horse, firing as the animal leaped forward. The horses crashed together, rearing, plunging, and Lockwood, as he felt the body of a man crush by him on the trail, clutched into the clothes of him, and, with the pistol pressed against the very flesh, fired again, crying out as he did so:

"Drop your gun, Reno! I know you. I'll kill you if you move again!"

And then it was that a wail rose into the night, a wail of agony and mortal apprehension:

"Signor Lockwude, Signor Lockwude, for the love of God, don't shoot! 'Tis I—Chino Zavalla."

VI

THE DISCOVERY OF FELICE

AN hour later, Felice, roused from her sleep by loud knocking upon her door, threw a blanket about her slim body, serape fashion, and opened the cabin to two gaunt scarecrows, who, the one, half supported by the other, himself far spent and all but swooning, lurched by her across the threshold and brought up wavering and bloody in the midst of the cabin floor.

"*Por Dios! Por Dios!*" cried Felice. "Ah, love of God! what misfortune has befallen Chino!" Then in English, and with a swift leap of surprise and dismay: "Ah, Meester Lockwude, air you hurt? Eh, tell me-a! Ah, it is too draidful!"

"No, no," gasped Lockwood, as he dragged Chino's unconscious body to the bed Felice had just left. "No; I—I've shot him. We met—there on the trail." Then the nerves that had stood strain already surprisingly long snapped and crisped back upon themselves like broken harp-strings.

55

"*I've shot him! I've shot him!*" he cried.
"Shot him, do you understand? Killed him,
it may be. Get the doctor, quick! He's at
the office. I passed Chino on the trail over to
the Hill. He'd hid in the bushes as he heard
me coming from behind, then when I came
back I took him. Oh, I'll explain later. Get
the doctor, quick."

Felice threw on such clothes as came to her
hand and ran over to the office, returning with
the doctor, half dressed and blinking in the
lantern-light. He went in to the wounded
man at once, and Lockwood, at the end of all
strength, dropped into the hammock on the
porch, stretching out his leg to ease the anguish
of his broken foot. He leaned back and closed
his eyes wearily, aware only of a hideous swirl
of pain, of intolerable anxiety as to Chino's
wound, and, most of all, of a mere blur of
confusion wherein the sights and sounds of
the last few hours tore through his brain with
the plunge of a wild galloping such as seemed
to have been in his ears for years and years.

But as he lay thus he heard a step at his
side. Then came the touch of Felice's long
brown hand upon his face. He sat up, opening
his eyes.

"You aisk me-a," she said, "eef I do onderstaind, eh? Yais, I onderstaind. You—"

her voice was a whisper—"you shoot Chino, eh? I know. You do those thing' for me-a. I am note angri, no-a. You ver' sharp man, eh? All for love oaf Felice, eh? Now we be happi, maybe; now we git married soam day byne-by, eh? Ah, you one brave man, Signor Lockwude!"

She would have taken his hand, but Lockwood, the pain all forgot, the confusion all vanishing, was on his feet. It was as though a curtain that for months had hung between him and the blessed light of clear understanding had suddenly been rent in twain by her words. The woman stood revealed. All the baseness of her tribe, all the degraded savagery of a degenerate race, all the capabilities for wrong, for sordid treachery, that lay dormant in her, leaped to life at this unguarded moment, and in that new light, that now at last she had herself let in, stood pitilessly revealed, a loathsome thing, hateful as malevolence itself.

"What," shouted Lockwood, "you think —think that I—that I *could*—oh-h, it's monstrous—*you*——" He could find no words to voice his loathing. Swiftly he turned away from her, the last spark of an evil love dying down forever in his breast.

It was a transformation, a thing as sudden as a miracle, as conclusive as a miracle, and with all a miracle's sense of uplift and power. In a second of time the scales seemed to fall from the man's eyes, fetters from his limbs; he saw, and he was free.

At the door Lockwood met the doctor:

"Well?"

"He's all right; only a superficial wound. He'll recover. But you—how about you? All right? Well, that is a good hearing. You've had a lucky escape, my boy."

"I *have* had a lucky escape," shouted Lockwood. "You don't know just how lucky it was."

A BARGAIN WITH PEG-LEG

A BARGAIN WITH PEG-LEG

H EY, youse!" shouted the car-boy. He brought his trundling, jolting, loose-jointed car to a halt by the face of the drift. "Hey, youse!" he shouted again.

Bunt shut off the Burly air-drill and nodded. "Chaw," he remarked to me.

We clambered into the car, and, as the boy released the brake, rolled out into the main tunnel of the Big Dipple, and banged and bumped down the long incline that led to the mouth.

"Chaw" was dinner. It was one o'clock in the morning, and the men on the night shift were taking their midnight spell off. Bunt was back at his old occupation of miner, and I— the one loafer of all that little world of workers —had brought him a bottle of beer to go with the "chaw"; for Bunt and I were ancient friends.

As we emerged from the cool, cave-like dampness of the mine and ran out into the wonderful night air of the Sierra foothills, warm, dry, redolent of witch-hazel, the car-boy began to cough, and, after we had climbed

61

out of the car and had sat down on the embankment to eat and drink, Bunt observed:

"D'ye hear that bark? That kid's a one-lunger for fair. Which ain't no salubrious graft for him—this hiking cars about in the bowels of the earth. Some day he'll sure up an' quit. Ought to go down to Yuma a spell."

The engineer in the mill was starting the stamps. They got under way with broken, hiccoughing dislocations, bumping and stumbling like the hoofs of a group of horses on the cattle-deck in a gale. Then they jumped to a trot, then to a canter, and at last settled down to the prolonged roaring gallop that reverberated far off over the entire cañon.

"I knew a one-lunger once," Bunt continued, as he uncorked the bottle, "and the acquaintance was some distressful by reason of its bringing me into strained relations with a cow-rustlin', hair-liftin', only-one-born-in-captivity, man-eatin' brute of a one-legged Greaser which he was named Peg-leg Smith. He was shy a leg because of a shotgun that the other man thought wasn't loaded. And this here happens, lemme tell you, 'way down in the Panamint country, where they wasn't no doctor within twenty miles, and Peg-leg outs with his bowie and amputates that leg hisself, then later makes a wood stump outa a ole halter and a table-leg.

I guess the whole jing-bang of it turned his head, for he goes bad and loco thereafter, and begins shootin' and r'arin' up an' down the hull Southwest, a-roarin' and a-bellerin' and a-takin' on amazin'. We dasn't say boo to a yaller pup while he's round. I never see such mean blood. Jus' let the boys know that Peg-leg was anyways adjacent an' you can gamble they walked chalk.

"Y'see, this Peg-leg lay it out as how he couldn't abide no cussin' an' swearin'. He said if there was any tall talkin' done he wanted to do it. And he sure could. I've seed him hold on for six minutes by the watch an' never repeat hisself once. An' shoot! Say, lemme tell you he did for two Greasers once in a bar-room at La Paz, one in front o' him, t'other straight behind, *him* standing between with a gun in each hand, and shootin' both guns *at the same time*. Well, he was just a terror," declared Bunt, solemnly, "and when he was in real good form there wa'n't a man south o' Leadville dared to call his hand.

"Now, the way I met up with this skunkin' little dewdrop was this-like. It was at Yuma, at a time when I was a kid of about nineteen. It was a Sunday mornin'; Peg-leg was in town. He was asleep on a lounge in the back room o' Bud Overick's Grand Transcontinental Hotel.

(I used to guess Bud called it that by reason that it wa'n't grand, nor transcontinental, nor yet a hotel—it was a bar.) This was twenty year ago, and in those days I knowed a one-lunger in Yuma named Clarence. (He couldn't help that—he was a good kid—but his name *was* Clarence.) We got along first-rate. Yuma was a great consumptive place at that time. They used to come in on every train; yes, and go out, too—by freight.

"Well, findin' that they couldn't do much else than jes' sit around an' bark and keep their shawls tight, these 'ere chaps kinda drew together, and lay it out to meet every Sunday morning at Bud's to sorta talk it over and have a quiet game. One game they had that they played steady, an' when I drifted into Bud's that morning they was about a dozen of 'em at it—Clarence, too. When I came in, there they be, all sittin' in a circle round a table with a cigar box on it. They'd each put four bits into the box. That was the pot.

"A stranger wouldn't 'a' made nothin' very excitin' out of that game, nor yet would 'a' caught on to what it were. For them pore yaps jes' sat there, each with his little glass thermometer in his mouth, a-waitin' and a-waitin' and never sayin' a word. Then bimeby Bud, who's a-holdin' of the watch on 'em, sings out 'Time !' an' they all takes their thermometers out an' looks at 'em careful-like to see where they stand.

" 'Mine's ninety-nine,' says one.

"An' another says:

" 'Mine's a hundred.'

"An' Clarence pipes up—coughin' all the time:

" 'Mine's a hundred 'n one 'n 'alf.'

"An', no one havin' a higher tempriture than that, Clarence captures the pot. It was a queer kind o' game.

"Well, on that particular Sunday morning they's some unpleasantness along o' one o' the other one-lungers layin' it out as how Clarence had done some monkey-business to make his tempriture so high. It was said as how Clarence had took and drunk some hot tea afore comin' into the game at Bud's. They all began to discuss that same p'int.

"Naturally, they don't go at it polite, and to make their remarks p'inted they says a cuss-word occasional, and Clarence, bein' a high-steppin' gent as takes nobody's dust, slings it back some forceful.

"Then all at once they hears Peg-leg beller from where's he layin' on the lounge (they ain't figured on his bein' so contiguous), and he gives it to be understood, does Peg-leg, as how the next one-lunger that indulges in whatsoever profanity will lose his voice abrupt.

"They all drops out at that, bar the chap who had the next highest tempriture to Clarence. Him having missed the pot by only a degree or so is considerable sore.

"'Why,' says he, 'I've had a reg'lar *fever* since yesterday afternoon, an' only just dodged a hem'rage by a squeak. I'm all legitimate, I am; an' if you-alls misdoubts as how my tempriture ain't normal you kin jes' ask the doctor. I don't take it easy that a strappin', healthy gesabe whose case ain't nowheres near the hopeless p'int yet steps in here with a scalded mouth and plays it low.'

"Clarence he r'ars right up at that an' forgits about Peg-leg an' expresses doubts, not to say convictions, about the one-lunger's chances of salvation. He puts it all into about three words, an' just as quick as look at it we hears ol' Peg-leg's wooden stump a-comin'. We stampedes considerable prompt, but Clarence falls over a chair, an' before he kin get up Peg-leg has him by the windpipe.

"Now I ain't billin' myself as a all-round star hero an' general grand-stand man. But I was sure took with Clarence, an' I'd 'a' been real disappointed if Peg-leg 'ud a-killed him that morning—which he sure was tryin' to do when I came in for a few chips.

"I don' draw on Peg-leg, him being down on his knees over Clarence, an' his back turned, but without sensin' very much *what* I'm a-doin' of I grabs holt o' the first part o' Peg-leg that comes handy, which, so help me, Bob, is his old wooden leg. I starts to pull him off o' Clarence, but instead o' that I pulls off the wooden leg an' goes a-staggerin' back agin the wall with the thing in my fist.

"Y'know how it is now with a fightin' pup if you pull his tail while he's a-chawin' up the other pup. Ye can bat him over the head till you're tired, or kick him till you w'ars your boot out, an' he'll go right on chawin' the harder. But monkey with his tail an' he's that sensitive an' techy about it that he'll take a interest right off.

"Well, it were just so with Peg-leg—though I never knew it. Just by accident I'd laid holt of him where he was tender; an' when he felt that leg go—say, lemme tell you, he was some excited. He forgits all about Clarence, and he lines out for me, a-clawin' the air. Lucky he'd left his gun in the other room.

"Well, sir, y'ought to have seen him, a-hoppin' on one foot, and banging agin the furniture, jes' naturally black in the face

with rage, an' doin' his darnedest to lay
his hands on me, roarin' all the whiles like
a steer with a kinked tail.

"Well, I'm skeered, and I remarks that same
without shame. I'm skeered. I don't want
to come to no grapples with Peg-leg in his
wrath, an' I knows that so long as he can't
git his leg he can't take after me very fast.
Bud's saloon backs right up agin the bluff over
the river. So what do I do but heave that same
wooden leg through one o' the back windows,
an' down she goes (as I *thought*) mebbe seventy
feet into the cañon o' the Colorado? And
then, mister man, *I skins out—fast.*

"I takes me headlong flight by way o' the
back room and *on-root* pitches Peg-leg's gun
over into the cañon, too, an' then whips around
the corner of the saloon an' fetches out ag'in by
the street in front. With his gun gone an'
his leg gone, Peg-leg—so long's y'ain't within
arm's reach—is as harmless as a horned toad.
So I kinda hangs 'round the neighbourhood
jes' to see what-all mout turn up.

"Peg-leg, after hoppin' back to find that his
gun was gone, to look for his leg, comes out by
the front door, hoppin' from one chair to another,
an' seein' me standin' there across the street
makes remarks; an' he informs me that because
of this same little turn-up this mornin' I ain't

never goin' to live to grow hair on my face. His observations are that vigorous an' p'inted that I sure begin to see it that way, too, and I says to myself:

" 'Now you, Bunt McBride, you've cut it out for yourself good and hard, an' the rest o' your life ain't goin' to be free from nervousness. Either y'ought to 'a' let this here hell-roarin' maverick alone or else you should 'a' put him clean out o' business when you had holt o' his shootin'-iron. An' I ain't a bit happy.' And then jes' at this stage o' the proceedings occurs what youse 'ud call a diversion.

" It seemed that that wood stump didn't go clean to the river as I first figured, but stuck three-fourths the way down. An' a-course there's a fool half-breed kid who's got to chase after it, thinkin' to do Peg-leg a good turn.

" I don't know nothin' about this, but jes' stand there talkin' back to Peg-leg, an' pretendin' I ain't got no misgivings, when I sees this kid comin' a-cavoortin' an' a-cayoodlin' down the street with the leg in his hands, hollerin' out:

" 'Here's your leg, Mister Peg-leg! I went an' got it for you, Mister Peg-leg!'

" It ain't so likely that Peg-leg could 'a' caught me even if he'd had his leg, but I wa'n't takin' no chances. An' as Peg-leg starts for the kid I start, too—with my heart knockin' agin my front teeth, you can bet.

"I never knew how fast a man could hop till that mornin', an', lookin' at Peg-leg with the tail o' my eye as I ran, it seemed to me as how he was a-goin' over the ground like a ole he-kangaroo. But somehow he gets off his balance and comes down all of a smash like a rickety table, an' I reaches the kid first an' takes the leg away from him.

"I guess Peg-leg must 'a' begun to lay it out by then that I held a straight flush to his ace high, for he sits down on the edge of the side-walk an', being some winded, too, he just glares. Then byme-by he says:

"'You think you are some smart now, sonny, but I'm a-studyin' of your face so's I'll know who to look for when I git a new leg; an' believe me, I'll know it, m'son—yours and your friend's too' (he meant Clarence)—'an' I guess you'll both be kind o' sick afore I'm done with you. *You!*' he goes on, tremendous disgustful. 'You! an' them one-lungers a-swearin' an' a-cussin' an' bedamnin' an' bedevilin' one a-other. Ain't ye just ashamed o' yourselves?' (he thought I was a one-lunger, too); 'ain't ye ashamed—befoulin' your mouths, and dis-turbin' the peace along of a quiet Sunday mornin', an' you-alls waist over in your graves?

I'm fair sick o' my job,' he remarks, goin' kind
o' thoughtful. 'Ten years now I've been
range-ridin' all this yere ranch, a-doin' o' my
little feeble, or'nary best to clean out the
mouths o' you men an' purify the atmosphere
o' God's own country, but I ain't made *one*
convert. I've pounded 'em an' booted 'em,
an' busted 'em an' shot 'em up, an' they go on
cussin' each other out harder'n ever. I don't
know w'at all to do an' I sometimes gets plumb
discouraged-like.'

"Now, hearin' of him talk that-a-way, an'
a-knowin' of his weakness, I gits a idea. It's
a chanst and mebbee it don't pan out, but I
puts it up as a bluff. I don't want, you see,
to spend the rest o' my appointed time in this
yere vale o' tears a-dodgin' o' Peg-leg Smith,
an' in the end, after all, to git between the wind
and a forty-eight caliber do-good, sure not.
So I puts up a deal. Says I: 'Peg-leg, I'll
make a bargint along o' you. You lays it out
as how you ain't never converted nobody out
o' his swearin' habits. Now if you wants, 'ere's
a chanst. You gimmee your word as a gent
and a good-man-an'-true, as how you won't
never make no play to shoot me up, in nowise
whatsoever, so long as we both do live, an'
promise never to bust me, or otherwise, and
promise never to rustle me or interfere with

my life, liberty and pursuit o' happiness, an'
thereunto you set your seal an' may Lord 'a'
mercy on your soul—you promise that, an' I
will agree an' covenant with the party o' the
first part to abstain an' abjure, early or late,
dry or drinkin', in liquor or out, out o' luck or
in, rangin' or roundin', from all part an' parcel o'
profanity, cuss-words, little or big, several and
separate, bar none; this yere agreement to be
considered as bindin' an' obligatory till the
day o' your demise, decease or death. *There !'*
says I, 'there's a fair bargint put up between
man an' man, an' I puts it to you fair. You
comes in with a strong ante an' you gets a
genuine, guaranteed an' high-grade convert—
the real article. You stays out, an' not only
you loses a good chanst to cut off and dam up
as vigorous a stream o' profanity as is found
between here and Laredo, but you loses a hand-
made, copper-bound, steel-riveted, artificial
limb—which in five minutes o' time,' says I,
windin' up, 'will sure feed the fire. There's
the bargint.'

"Well, the ol' man takes out time for about
as long as a thirsty horse-rustler could put
away half a dozen drinks an' he studies the
proposition sideways and endways an' down
side up. Then at last he ups and speaks out
decided-like:

" 'Son,' he says, 'son, it's a bargint. Gimmee my leg.'

"Somehow neither o' us misdoubts as how the other man won't keep his word; an' I gives him his stump, an' he straps her on joyful-like, just as if he'd got back a ole friend. Then later on he hikes out for Mojave and I don' see him no more for mebbe three years."

"And then?" I prompted.

"Well, I'll tell you," continued Bunt, between mouthfuls of pie, "I'll tell you. This yere prejudice agin profanity is the only thing about this yere Peg-leg that ain't pizen bad, an' *that* prejudice, you got to know, was just along o' his being loco on that one subjeck. 'Twa'n't as if he had any real principles or convictions about the thing. It was just a loco prejudice. Just as some gesabes has feelin's agin cats an' snakes, or agin seein' a speckled nigger. It was just on-reasonable. So what I'm aimin' to have you understand is the fact that it was extremely appropriate that Peg-leg should die, that it was a blame good thing, and somethin' to be celebrated by free drinks all round.

"You can say he treated me white, an' took my unsupported word. Well, so he did; but that was in spite o' what he really was hisself, 'way on the inside o' him. Inside o' him he was black-bad, an' it wa'n't a week after we

had made our bargint that he did for a little
Mojave kid in a way I don't like to think of.

"So when he took an' died like as how I'm
a-going to tell you of, I was plumb joyful, not
only because I could feel at liberty to relieve
my mind when necessary in a manner as is
approved of and rightful among gents—not
only because o' that, but because they was one
less bad egg in the cow-country.

"Now the manner o' Peg-leg's dying was sure
hilarious-like. I didn't git over laughin' about
it for a month o' Sundays—an' I ain't done
yet. It was sure a joke on Peg-leg. The
cutest joke that ever was played off on him.

"It was in Sonora—Sonora, Arizona, I mean.
They'd a-been a kind o' gold excitement there,
and all the boys had rounded up. The town
was full—chock-a-block. Peg-leg he was there
too, drunk all the time an' bullyin' everybody,
an' slambangin' around in his same old way.
That very day he'd used a friend o' his—his
best friend—cruel hard: just mean and nasty,
you know.

"Well, I'm sitting into a little game o' faro
about twelve o'clock at night, me an' about a
dozen o' the boys. We're good an' interested,
and pretty much to the good o' the game, an'
somebody's passin' drinks when all at once
there's a sure big rumpus out in the street,

an' a gent sticks his head thro' the door
an' yells out:

"'Hi, there, they's a fire! The Golden West
Hotel is on fire!'

"We draws the game as soon as convenient
and hikes out, an', my word, you'd 'a' thought
from the looks o' things as how the whole town
was going. But it was only the hotel—the
Golden West, where Peg-leg was stayin'; an'
when we got up we could hear the ol' murderer
bellerin' an' ragin', an' him drunk—of course.

"Well, I'm some excited. Lord love you,
I'd as soon 'a' seen Peg-leg shot as I would eat,
an' when I remembers the little Mojave kid
I'm glad as how his time is at hand. Saved
us the trouble o' lynchin' that sooner or later
had to come.

"Peg-leg's room was in the front o' the house
on the fourth floor, but the fire was all below,
and what with the smoke comin' out the third-
story winders he couldn't see down into the
street, no more'n the boys could see him—only
they just heard him bellerin'.

"Then some one of 'em sings out:

"'Hey, Peg-leg, jump! We got a blanket
here.'

"An' sure enough he does jump!"

Here Bunt chuckled grimly, muttering,
"Yes, sir, sure enough he did jump."

"I don't quite see," I observed, "where the laugh comes in. What was the joke of it?"

"The joke of it was," finished Bunt, "that they hadn't any blanket."

THE PASSING OF COCK-EYE
BLACKLOCK

THE PASSING OF COCK-EYE BLACKLOCK

WELL, m'son," observed Bunt about half an hour after supper, "if your provender has shook down comfortable by now, we might as well jar loose and be moving along out yonder."

We left the fire and moved toward the hobbled ponies, Bunt complaining of the quality of the outfit's meals. "Down in the Panamint country," he growled, "we had a Chink that was a sure frying-pan expert; but *this* Dago— my word! That ain't victuals, that supper That's just a' ingenious device for removing superfluous appetite. Next time I assimilate nutriment in this camp I'm sure going to take chloroform beforehand. Careful to draw your cinch tight on that pinto bronc' of yours. She always swells up same as a horned toad soon as you begin to saddle up."

We rode from the circle of the camp-fire's light and out upon the desert. It was Bunt's turn to ride the herd that night, and I had volunteered to bear him company.

Bunt was one of a fast-disappearing type. He knew his West as the cockney knows his

Piccadilly. He had mined with and for Ralston, had soldiered with Crook, had turned cards in a faro game at Laredo, and had known the Apache Kid. He had fifteen separate and different times driven the herds from Texas to Dodge City, in the good old, rare old, wild old days when Dodge was the headquarters for the cattle trade, and as near to heaven as the cowboy cared to get. He had seen the end of gold and the end of the buffalo, the beginning of cattle, the beginning of wheat, and the spreading of the barbed-wire fence, that, in the end, will take from him his occupation and his revolver, his chaparejos and his usefulness, his lariat and his reason for being. He had seen the rise of a new period, the successive stages of which, singularly enough, tally exactly with the progress of our own world-civilization: first the nomad and hunter, then the herder, next and last the husbandman. He had passed the mid-mark of his life. His mustache was gray. He had four friends —his horse, his pistol, a teamster in the Indian Territory Panhandle named Skinny, and me.

The herd—I suppose all told there were some two thousand head—we found not far from the water-hole. We relieved the other watch and took up our night's vigil. It was about nine o'clock. The night was fine, calm.

There was no cloud. Toward the middle watches one could expect a moon. But the stars, the stars! In Idaho, on those lonely reaches of desert and range, where the shadow of the sun by day and the courses of the constellations by night are the only things that move, these stars are a different matter from those bleared pin-points of the city after dark, seen through dust and smoke and the glare of electrics and the hot haze of fire-signs. On such a night as that when I rode the herd with Bunt *anything* might have happened; one could have believed in fairies then, and in the buffalo-ghost, and in all the weirds of the craziest Apache "Messiah" that ever made medicine.

One remembered astronomy and the "measureless distances" and the showy problems, including the rapid moving of a ray of light and the long years of its travel between star and star, and smiled incredulously. Why, the stars were just above our heads, were not much higher than the flat-topped hills that barred the horizons. Venus was a yellow lamp hung in a tree; Mars a red lantern in a clock-tower.

One listened instinctively for the tramp of the constellations. Orion, Cassiopeia and Ursa Major marched to and fro on the vault

like cohorts of legionaries, seemingly within
call of our voices, and all without a sound.

But beneath these quiet heavens the earth
disengaged multitudinous sounds—small sounds,
minimized as it were by the muffling of the
night. Now it was the yap of a coyote
leagues away; now the snapping of a twig in
the sage-brush; now the mysterious, indefinable
stir of the heat-ridden land cooling under the
night. But more often it was the confused
murmur of the herd itself—the click of a horn,
the friction of heavy bodies, the stamp of a
hoof, with now and then the low, complaining
note of a cow with a calf, or the subdued noise
of a steer as it lay down, first lurching to the
knees, then rolling clumsily upon the
haunch, with a long, stertorous breath of satis-
faction.

Slowly at Indian trot we encircle the herd.
Earlier in the evening a prairie-wolf had
pulled down a calf, and the beasts were still
restless.

Little eddies of nervousness at long intervals
developed here and there in the mass—eddies
that not impossibly might widen at any time
with perilous quickness to the maelstrom of a
stampede. So as he rode Bunt sang to these
great brutes, literally to put them to sleep—
sang an old grandmother's song, with all the

quaint modulations of sixty, seventy, a hundred years ago:

> " With her ogling winks
> And bobbling blinks,
> Her quizzing glass,
> Her one eye idle,
> Oh, she loved a bold dragoon,
> With his broadsword, saddle, bridle.
> *Whack*, fol-de-rol !"

I remember that song. My grandmother—so they tell me—used to sing it in Carolina, in the thirties, accompanying herself on a harp, if you please:

> "Oh, she loved a bold dragoon,
> With his broadsword, saddle, bridle. "

It was in Charleston, I remembered, and the slave-ships used to discharge there in those days. My grandmother had sung it then to her beaux; officers they were; no wonder she chose it—"Oh, she loved a bold dragoon"—and now I heard it sung on an Idaho cattle-range to quiet two thousand restless steers.

Our talk at first, after the cattle had quieted down, ran upon all manner of subjects. It is astonishing to note what strange things men will talk about at night and in a solitude. That night we covered religion, of course, astronomy, love affairs, horses, travel, history, poker, photography, basket-making, and the Darwinian theory. But at last inevitably we came back to cattle and the pleasures and dangers of riding the herd.

"I rode herd once in Nevada," remarked Bunt, "and I was caught into a blizzard, and I was sure freezing to death. Got to where I couldn't keep my eyes open, I was that sleepy. Tell you what I did. Had some eating-tobacco along, and I'd chew it a spell, then rub the juice into my eyes. Kept it up all night. Blame near blinded me, but I come through. Me and another man named Blacklock—Cock-eye Blacklock we called him, by reason of his having one eye that was some out of line. Cock-eye sure ought to have got it that night, for he went bad afterward, and did a heap of killing before he *did* get it. He was a bad man for sure, and the way he died is a story in itself."

There was a long pause. The ponies jogged on. Rounding on the herd, we turned southward.

"He did 'get it' finally, you say," I prompted.

"He certainly did," said Bunt, "and the story of it is what a man with a' imaginary mind like you ought to make into one of your friction tales."

"Is it about a treasure?" I asked with apprehension. For ever since I once made a tale (of friction) out of one of Bunt's stories of real life, he has been ambitious for me to

write another, and is forever suggesting motifs
which invariably—I say invariably—imply
the discovery of great treasures. With him,
fictitious literature must always turn upon the
discovery of hidden wealth.

"No," said he, "it ain't about no treasure,
but just about the origin, hist'ry and development—and subsequent decease—of as mean a
Greaser as ever stole stock, which his name was
Cock-eye Blacklock.

"You see, this same Blacklock went bad
about two summers after out meet-up with the
blizzard. He worked down Yuma way and
over into New Mexico, where he picks up with
a sure-thing gambler, and the two begin to
devastate the population. They do say when
he and his running mate got good and through
with that part of the Land of the Brave, men
used to go round trading guns for commissary,
and clothes for ponies, and cigars for whisky
and such. There just wasn't any money left
anywhere. Those sharps had drawed the landscape clean. Some one found a dollar in a
floor-crack in a saloon, and the barkeep' gave
him a gallon of forty-rod for it, and used to
keep it in a box for exhibition, and the crowd
would get around it and paw it over and say:
'My! my! Whatever in the world is this extremely cu-roos coin?'

"Then Blacklock cuts loose from his running mate, and plays a lone hand through Arizona and Nevada, up as far as Reno again, and there he stacks up against a kid—a little tenderfoot kid so new he ain't cracked the green paint off him—and *skins* him. And the kid, being foolish and impulsive-like, pulls out a pea-shooter. It was a *twenty-two*," said Bunt, solemnly. "Yes, the kid was just that pore, pathetic kind to carry a dinky twenty-two, and with the tears runnin' down his cheeks begins to talk tall. Now what does that Cock-eye do? Why, that pore kid that he had skinned couldn't 'a' hurt him with his pore little bric-à-brac. Does Cock-eye take his little parlour ornament away from him, and spank him, and tell him to go home? No, he never. The kid's little tin pop-shooter explodes right in his hand before he can crook his forefinger twice, and while he's a-wondering what-all has happened Cock-eye gets his two guns on him, slow and deliberate like, mind you, and throws forty-eights into him till he ain't worth shooting at no more. Murders him like the mud-eating, horse-thieving snake of a Greaser that he is; but being within the law, the kid drawing on him first, he don't stretch hemp the way he should.

"Well, fin'ly this Blacklock blows into a mining-camp in Placer County, California, where I'm chuck-tending on the night-shift. This here camp is maybe four miles across the divide from Iowa Hill, and it sure is named a cu-roos name, which it is Why-not. They is a barn contiguous, where the mine horses are kep', and, blame me! if there ain't a weather-cock on top of that same—a golden trotting-horse—*upside down*. When the stranger an' pilgrim comes in, says he first off: 'Why'n snakes they got that weathercock horse upside down—why?' says he. 'Why-not,' says you, and the drinks is on the pilgrim.

"That all went very lovely till some gesabe opens up a placer drift on the far side the divide, starts a rival camp, an' names her Because. The Boss gets mad at that, and rights up the weathercock, and renames the camp Ophir, and you don't work no more pilgrims.

"Well, as I was saying, Cock-eye drifts into Why-not and begins diffusing trouble. He skins some of the boys in the hotel over in town, and a big row comes of it, and one of the bed-rock cleaners cuts loose with both guns. Nobody hurt but a quarter-breed, who loses a' eye. But the marshal don't stand for no short-card men, an' closes Cock-eye up some prompt. Him being forced to give the boys back their money is busted an' can't get away from camp. To raise some wind he begins depredating.

"He robs a pore half-breed of a cayuse, and shoots up a Chink who's panning tailings, and generally and variously becomes too pronounced, till he's run outen camp. He's sure stony-broke, not being able to turn a card because of the marshal. So he goes to live in a ole cabin up by the mine ditch, and sits there doing a heap o' thinking, and hatching trouble like a' ole he-hen.

"Well, now, with that deporting of Cock-eye comes his turn of bad luck, and it sure winds his clock up with a loud report. I've narrated special of the scope and range of this 'ere Blacklock, so as you'll understand why it was expedient and desirable that he should up an' die. You see, he always managed, with all his killings and robbings and general and sundry flimflamming, to be just within the law. And if anybody took a notion to shoot him up, why, his luck saw him through, and the other man's shooting-iron missed fire, or exploded, cr threw wild, or such like, till it seemed as if he sure did bear a charmed life; and so he did till a pore yeller tamale of a fool dog did for him what the law of the land couldn't do. Yes, sir, a fool dog, a pup, a blame yeller pup named Sloppy Weather, did for Cock-eye Blacklock, sporting character, three-card-monte man, sure-thing sharp, killer, and general bedeviler.

" You see, it was this way. Over in American Cañon, some five miles maybe back of the mine, they was a creek called the American River, and it was sure chock-a-block full of trouts. The Boss used for to go over there with a dinky fish-pole like a buggy-whip about once a week, and scout that stream for fish and bring back a basketful. He was sure keen on it, and had bought some kind of privilege or other, so as he could keep other people off.

" Well, I used to go along with him to pack the truck, and one Saturday, about a month after Cock-eye had been run outen camp, we hiked up over the divide, and went for to round up a bunch o' trouts. When we got to the river there was a mess for your life. Say, that river was full of dead trouts, floating atop the water; and they was some even on the bank. Not a scratch on 'em; just dead. The Boss had the papsy-lals. I never *did* see a man so rip-r'aring, snorting mad. *I* hadn't a guess about what we were up against, but he knew, and he showed down. He said somebody had been shooting the river for fish to sell down Sacramento way to the market. A mean trick; kill more fish in one shoot than you can possibly pack.

"Well, we didn't do much fishing that day—couldn't get a bite, for that matter—and took off home about noon to talk it over.   You see, the Boss, in buying the privileges or such for that creek, had made himself responsible to the Fish Commissioners of the State, and 'twasn't a week before they were after him, camping on his trail incessant, and wanting to know how about it.   The Boss was some worried, because the fish were being killed right along, and the Commission was making him weary of living. Twicet afterward we prospected along that river and found the same lot of dead fish.   We even put a guard there, but it didn't do no manner of good.

"It's the Boss who first suspicions Cock-eye. But it don't take no seventh daughter of no seventh daughter to trace trouble where Black-lock's about.   He sudden shows up in town with a bunch of simoleons, buying bacon and tin cows* and such provender, and generally giving it away that he's come into money. The Boss, who's watching his movements sharp, says to me one day:

"'Bunt, the storm-centre of this here low area is a man with a cock-eye, an' I'll back that play with a paint horse against a paper dime.'

* Condensed milk.

"'No takers,' says I. 'Dirty work and a cock-eyed man are two heels of the same mule.'

"'Which it's a-kicking of me in the stummick frequent and painful,' he remarks, plenty wrathful.

"'On general principles,' I said, 'it's a royal flush to a pair of deuces as how this Blacklock bird ought to stop a heap of lead, and I know the man to throw it. He's the only brother of my sister, and tends chuck in a placer mine. How about if I take a day off and drop round to his cabin and interview him on the fleetin' and unstable nature of human life?'

"But the Boss wouldn't hear of that.

"'No,' says he; 'that's not the bluff to back in this game. You an' me an' Mary-go-round'—that was what we called the marshal, him being so much all over the country—'you an' me an' Mary-go-round will have to stock a sure-thing deck against that maverick.'

"So the three of us gets together an' has a talky-talk, an' we lays it out as how Cock-eye must be watched and caught red-handed.

"Well, let me tell you, keeping case on that Greaser sure did lack a certain indefinable charm. We tried him at sun-up, an' again at sundown, an' nights, too, laying in the chaparral an' tarweed, an' scouting up an' down that blame river, till we were sore. We built

surreptitious a lot of shooting-boxes up in trees
on the far side of the cañon, overlooking certain
an' sundry pools in the river where Cock-eye
would be likely to pursue operations, an' we
took turns watching.   I'll be a Chink if that
bad egg didn't put it on us same as previous,
an' we'd find new-killed fish all the time.   I
tell you we were *fitchered;* and it got on the
Boss's nerves.   The Commission began to talk
of withdrawing the privilege, an' it was up
to him to make good or pass the deal.   We
knew Blacklock was shooting the river, y' see,
but we didn't have no evidence.   Y' see, being
shut off from card-sharping, he was up against
it, and so took to pot-hunting to get along.
It was as plain as red paint.

"Well, things went along sort of catch-as-
catch-can like this for maybe three weeks, the
Greaser shooting fish regular, an' the Boss
b'iling with rage, and laying plans to call his
hand, and getting bluffed out every deal.

"And right here I got to interrupt, to talk
some about the pup dog, Sloppy Weather.   If
he hadn't got caught up into this Blacklock
game, no one'd ever thought enough about him
to so much as kick him.   But after it was all
over, we began to remember this same Sloppy
an' to recall what he was; no big job.   He was
just a worthless fool pup, yeller at that, every-

body's dog, that just hung round camp, grinning and giggling and playing the goat, as halfgrown dogs will. He used to go along with the car-boys when they went swimmin' in the resevoy, an' dash along in an' yell an' splash round just to show off. He thought it was a keen stunt to get some gesabe to throw a stick in the resevoy so's he could paddle out after it. They'd trained him always to bring it back an' fetch it to whichever party throwed it. He'd give it up when he'd retrieved it, an' yell to have it throwed again. That was his idea of fun—just like a fool pup.

"Well, one day this Sloppy Weather is off chasing jack-rabbits an' don't come home. Nobody thinks anything about that, nor even notices it. But we afterward finds out that he'd met up with Blacklock that day, an' stopped to visit with him—sorry day for Cockeye. Now it was the very next day after this that Mary-go-round an' the Boss plans another scout. I'm to go, too. It was a Wednesday, an' we lay it out that the Cockeye would prob'ly shoot that day so's to get his fish down to the railroad Thursday, so they'd reach Sacramento Friday—fish day, see. It wasn't much to go by, but it was the high card in our hand, an' we allowed to draw to it.

"We left Why-not afore daybreak, an'

worked over into the cañon about sun-up.
They was one big pool we hadn't covered for
some time, an' we made out we'd watch that.
So we worked down to it, an' clumb up into our
trees, an' set out to keep guard.

"In about an hour we heard a shoot some
mile or so up the creek. They's no mistaking
dynamite, leastways not to miners, an' we
knew that shoot was dynamite an' nothing
else. The Cock-eye was at work, an' we shook
hands all round. Then pretty soon a fish or
so began to go by—big fellows, some of 'em,
dead an' floatin', with their eyes popped 'way
out same as knobs—sure sign they'd been shot.

"The Boss took and grit his teeth when he
see a three-pounder go by, an' made remarks
about Blacklock.

"' 'Sh!' says Mary-go-round, sudden-like.
'Listen!'

"We turned ear down the wind, an' sure there
was the sound of some one scrabbling along
the boulders by the riverside. Then we heard
a pup yap.

"' That's our man,' whispers the Boss.

"For a long time we thought Cock-eye had
quit for the day an' had coppered us again,
but byne-by we heard the manzanita crack on
the far side the cañon, an' there at last we see
Blacklock working down toward the pool,

Sloppy Weather following an' yapping and cayoodling just as a fool dog will.

"Blacklock comes down to the edge of the water quiet-like. He lays his big scoop-net an' his sack—we can see it half full already—down behind a boulder, and takes a good squinting look all round, and listens maybe twenty minutes, he's that cute, same's a coyote stealing sheep. We lies low an' says nothing, fear he might see the leaves move.

"Then byne-by he takes his stick of dynamite out his hip pocket—he was just that reckless kind to carry it that way—an' ties it careful to a couple of stones he finds handy. Then he lights the fuse an' heaves her into the drink, an' just there's where Cock-eye makes the mistake of his life. He ain't tied the rocks tight enough, an' the loop slips off just as he swings back his arm, the stones drop straight down by his feet, and the stick of dynamite whirls out right enough into the pool.

"Then the funny business begins.

"Blacklock ain't made no note of Sloppy Weather, who's been sizing up the whole game an' watchin' for the stick. Soon as Cock-eye heaves the dynamite into the water, off goes the pup after it, just as he'd been taught to do by the car-boys.

"'Hey, you fool dog!' yells Blacklock.

"A lot that pup cares. He heads out for
that stick of dynamite same as if for a veal
cutlet, reaches it, grabs hold of it, an' starts
back for shore, with the fuse sputterin' like hot
grease. Blacklock heaves rocks at him like
one possessed, capering an' dancing; but the
pup comes right on. The Cock-eye can't stand
it no longer, but lines out. But the pup's got
to shore an' takes after him. Sure; why not?
He think's it's all part of the game. Takes
after Cock-eye, running to beat a' express,
while we-all whoops and yells an' nearly falls
out the trees for laffing. Hi! Cock-eye did
scratch gravel for sure. But 'tain't no manner
of use. He can't run through that rough
ground like Sloppy Weather, an' that fool pup
comes a-cavartin' along, jumpin' up against
him, an' him a-kickin' him away, an' r'arin', an'
dancin', an' shakin' his fists, an' the more he
r'ars the more fun the pup thinks it is. But
all at once something big happens, an' the
whole bank of the cañon opens out like a big
wave, and slops over into the pool, an' the air
is full of trees an' rocks and cart-loads of dirt
an' dogs and Blacklocks and rivers an' smoke
an' fire generally. The Boss got a clod o'
river-mud spang in the eye, an' went off his
limb like's he was trying to bust a bucking
bronc' an' couldn't; and ol' Mary-go-round was

shooting off his gun on general principles, glarin' round wild-eyed an' like as if he saw a' Injun devil.

"When the smoke had cleared away an' the trees and rocks quit falling, we clumb down from our places an' started in to look for Blacklock. We found a good deal of him, but they wasn't hide nor hair left of Sloppy Weather. We didn't have to dig no grave, either. They was a big enough hole in the ground to bury a horse an' wagon, let alone Cock-eye. So we planted him there, an' put up a board, an' wrote on it:

Here lies most
of
C. BLACKLOCK,
who died of a'
entangling alliance with
a
stick of dynamite.

Moral: A hook and line is good enough
fish-tackle for any honest man.

"That there board lasted for two years, till the freshet of '82, when the American River—— Hello, there's the sun!"

All in a minute the night seemed to have closed up like a great book. The East flamed roseate. The air was cold, nimble. Some of the sage-brush bore a thin rim of frost. The herd, aroused, the dew glistening on flank and horn, were chewing the first cud of the day,

and in twos and threes moving toward the
water-hole for the morning's drink. Far off
toward the camp the breakfast fire sent a shaft
of blue smoke straight into the moveless air.
A jack-rabbit, with erect ears, limped from the
sage-brush just out of pistol-shot and regarded
us a moment, his nose wrinkling and trembling.
By the time that Bunt and I, putting our
ponies to a canter, had pulled up by the camp
of the Bar-circle-Z outfit, another day had
begun in Idaho.

A MEMORANDUM OF SUDDEN
DEATH

A MEMORANDUM OF SUDDEN DEATH

THE manuscript of the account that follows belongs to a harness-maker in Albuquerque, Juan Tejada by name, and he is welcome to whatever of advertisement this notice may bring him. He is a good fellow, and his patented martingale for stage horses may be recommended. I understand he got the manuscript from a man named Bass, or possibly Bass left it with him for safe-keeping. I know that Tejada has some things of Bass's now—things that Bass left with him last November: a mess-kit, a lantern and a broken theodolite—a whole saddle-box full of contraptions. I forgot to ask Tejada how Bass got the manuscript, and I wish I had done so now, for the finding of it might be a story itself. The probabilities are that Bass simply picked it up page by page off the desert, blown about the spot where the fight occurred and at some little distance from the bodies. Bass, I am told, is a bone-gatherer by profession, and one can easily understand how he would come across the scene of the encounter in one of his tours into western Arizona. My interest in

the affair is impersonal, but none the less keen.
Though I did not know young Karslake, I
knew his stuff—as everybody still does, when
you come to that. For the matter of that,
the mere mention of his pen-name, "Anson
Qualtraugh," recalls at once to thousands of
the readers of a certain world-famous monthly
magazine of New York articles and stories he
wrote for it while he was alive; as, for instance,
his admirable descriptive work called "Traces
of the Aztecs on the Mogolon Mesa," in the
October number of 1890. Also, in the January
issue of 1892 there are two specimens of his
work, one signed Anson Qualtraugh and the
other Justin Blisset. Why he should have
used the Blisset signature I do not know. It
occurs only this once in all his writings. In
this case it is signed to a very indifferent New
Year's story. The Qualtraugh "stuff" of the
same number is, so the editor writes to me,
a much shortened transcript of a monograph
on "Primitive Methods of Moki Irrigation,"
which are now in the archives of the Smith-
sonian. The admirable novel, "The Peculiar
Treasure of Kings," is of course well known.
Karslake wrote it in 1888–89, and the contro-
versy that arose about the incident of the
third chapter is still—sporadically and inter-
mittently—continued.

The manuscript that follows now appears, of course, for the first time in print, and I acknowledge herewith my obligations to Karslake's father, Mr. Patterson Karslake, for permission to publish.

I have set the account down word for word, with all the hiatuses and breaks that by nature of the extraordinary circumstances under which it was written were bound to appear in it. I have allowed it to end precisely as Karslake was forced to end it, in the middle of a sentence. God knows the real end is plain enough and was not far off when the poor fellow began the last phrase that never was to be finished.

The value of the thing is self-apparent. Besides the narrative of incidents it is a simple setting forth of a young man's emotions in the very face of violent death. You will remember the distinguished victim of the guillotine, a lady who on the scaffold begged that she might be permitted to write out the great thoughts that began to throng her mind. She was not allowed to do so, and the record is lost. Here is a case where the record is preserved. But Karslake, being a young man not very much given to introspection, his work is more a picture of things seen than a transcription of things thought. However, one may read between the lines; the very breaks are eloquent,

while the break at the end speaks with a significance that no words could attain.

The manuscript in itself is interesting. It
is written partly in pencil, partly in ink (no
doubt from a fountain pen), on sheets of manila
paper torn from some sort of long and narrow
account-book. In two or three places there
are smudges where the powder-blackened finger
and thumb held the sheets momentarily. I
would give much to own it, but Tejada will
not give it up without Bass's permission, and
Bass has gone to the Klondike.

As to Karslake himself. He was born in
Raleigh, in North Carolina, in 1868, studied
law at the State University, and went to the
Bahamas in 1885 with the members of a government coast survey commission. Gave up the
practice of law and "went in" for fiction and
the study of the ethnology of North America
about 1887. He was unmarried.

The reasons for his enlisting have long been
misunderstood. It was known that at the
time of his death he was a member of B Troop
of the Sixth Regiment of United States Cavalry,
and it was assumed that because of this fact
Karslake was in financial difficulties and not
upon good terms with his family. All this, of
course, is untrue, and I have every reason to
believe that Karslake at this time was planning

a novel of military life in the Southwest, and, wishing to get in closer touch with the *milieu* of the story, actually enlisted in order to be able to write authoritatively. He saw no active service until the time when his narrative begins. The year of his death is uncertain. It was in the spring probably of 1896, in the twenty-eighth year of his age.

There is no doubt he would have become in time a great writer. A young man of twenty-eight who had so lively a sense of the value of accurate observation, and so eager a desire to produce that in the very face of death he could faithfully set down a description of his surroundings, actually laying down the rifle to pick up the pen, certainly was possessed of extraordinary faculties.

"They came in sight early this morning just after we had had breakfast and had broken camp. The four of us—'Bunt,' 'Idaho,' Estorijo and myself—were jogging on to the southward and had just come up out of the dry bed of some water-hole—the alkali was white as snow in the crevices —when Idaho pointed them out to us, three to the rear, two on one side, one on the other and—very far away—two ahead. Five minutes before, the desert was as empty

as the flat of my hand. They seemed literally
to have *grown* out of the sage-brush. We took
them in through my field-glasses and Bunt
made sure they were an outlying band of Hunt-
in-the-Morning's Bucks. I had thought, and
so had all of us, that the rest of the boys had
rounded up the whole of the old man's hostiles
long since. We are at a loss to account for
these fellows here. They seem to be well
mounted.

"We held a council of war from the saddle
without halting, but there seemed very little
to be done—but to go right along and wait for
developments. At about eleven we found
water—just a pocket in the bed of a dried
stream—and stopped to water the ponies. I
am writing this during the halt.

"We have one hundred and sixteen rifle
cartridges. Yesterday was Friday, and all
day, as the newspapers say, 'the situation
remained unchanged.' We expected surely
that the night would see some rather radical
change, but nothing happened, though we
stood watch and watch till morning. Of yesterday's eight only six are in sight and we
bring up reserves. We now have two to the
front, one on each side, and two to the rear, all
far out of rifle-range.

[*The following paragraph is in an unsteady*

*script and would appear to have been written
in the saddle. The same peculiarity occurs
from time to time in the narrative, and occasion-
ally the writing is so broken as to be illegible.*]

"On again after breakfast. It is about
eight-fifteen. The other two have come back—
without 'reserves,' thank God. Very possibly
they did not go away at all, but were hidden
by a dip in the ground. I cannot see that any
of them are nearer. I have watched one to the
left of us steadily for more than half an
hour and I am sure that he has not shortened
the distance between himself and us.
What their plans are Hell only knows, but
this silent, persistent escorting tells on
the nerves. I do not think I am afraid—
as yet. It does not seem possible but that
we will ride into La Paz at the end of the
fortnight exactly as we had planned, meet
Greenock according to arrangements and take
the stage on to the railroad. Then next month
I shall be in San Antonio and report at headquarters. Of course, all this is to be, of course;
and this business of to-day will make a good
story to tell. It's an experience—good 'ma-
terial.' Very naturally I cannot now see how I
am going to get out of this" [*the word "alive"
has here been erased*], "but of course I *will*. Why
'of course'? I don't know. Maybe I am try-

ing to deceive myself. Frankly, it looks like a situation insoluble; but the solution will surely come right enough in good time.

" Eleven o'clock.—No change.

" Two-thirty P. M.—We are halted to tighten girths and to take a single swallow of the canteens. One of them rode in a wide circle from the rear to the flank, about ten minutes ago, conferred a moment with his fellow, then fell back to his old position. He wears some sort of red cloth or blanket. We reach no more water till day after to-morrow. But we have sufficient. Estorijo has been telling funny stories en route.

" Four o'clock P. M.—They have closed up perceptibly, and we have been debating about trying one of them with Idaho's Winchester. No use; better save the ammunition. It looks . . ." [*the next words are undecipherable, but from the context they would appear to be* "*as if they would attack to-night*"] " . . . we have come to know certain of them now by nicknames. We speak of the Red One, or the Little One, or the One with the Feather, and Idaho has named a short thickset fellow on our right 'Little Willie.' By God, I wish something would turn up—relief or fight. I don't care which. How Estorijo can cackle on, reeling off his senseless, pointless funny stories, is beyond me. Bunt is almost as bad. They understand the fix we are in, I *know*, but how they can take it so easily is the staggering surprise. I feel that I am as courageous as either of them, but levity seems horribly inappropriate. I could kill Estorijo joyfully.

"Sunday morning.—Still no developments. We were so sure of something turning up last night that none of us pretended to sleep. But nothing stirred. There is no sneaking out of the circle at night. The moon is full. A jack-rabbit could not have slipped by them unseen last night.

"Nine o'clock (in the saddle).—We had coffee and bacon as usual at sunrise; then on again to the southeast just as before. For half an hour after starting the Red One and two others were well within rifle-shot, nearer than ever before. They had worked in from the flank. But before Idaho could get a chance at them they dipped into a shallow arroyo, and when they came out on the other side were too far away to think of shooting.

"Ten o'clock.—All at once we find there are nine instead of eight; where and when this last one joined the band we cannot tell. He wears a sombrero and army trousers, but the upper part of his body is bare. Idaho calls him 'Half-and-half.' He is riding a—— They're coming.

"Later.—For a moment we thought it was
the long-expected rush.   The Red One—he had
been in the front—wheeled quick as a flash
and came straight for us, and the others followed
suit.   Great Heavens, how they rode! We
could hear them yelling on every side of us.
We jumped off our ponies and stood behind
them, the rifles across the saddles.   But at
four hundred yards they all pivoted about and
cantered off again leisurely.   Now they followed us as before—three in the front, two in
the rear and two on either side.   I do not think
I am going to be frightened when the rush does
come.   I watched myself just now.   I was
excited, and I remember Bunt saying to me,
'Keep your shirt on, m'son'; but I was not
afraid of being killed.   Thank God for that!
It is something I've long wished to find out,
and now that I know it I am proud of it.
Neither side fired a shot.   I was not afraid.
It's glorious.   Estorijo is all right.

"Sunday afternoon, one-thirty.—No change.
It is unspeakably hot.

"Three-fifteen.—The One with the Feather
is walking, leading his pony.   It seems to be
lame." [*With this entry Karslake ended page
five, and the next page of the manuscript is
numbered seven.   It is very probable, however,
that he made a mistake in the numerical sequence*

of his pages, for the narrative is continuous, and, at this point at least, unbroken. There does not seem to be any sixth page.]

"Four o'clock.—Is it possible that we are to pass another night of suspense? They certainly show no signs of bringing on the crisis, and they surely would not attempt anything so late in the afternoon as this. It is a relief to feel that we have nothing to fear till morning, but the tension of watching all night long is fearful.

"Later.—Idaho has just killed the Little One.

"Later.—Still firing.

"Later.—Still at it.

"Later, about five.—A bullet struck within three feet of me.

"Five-ten.—Still firing.

"Seven-thirty P. M., in camp.—It happened so quickly that it was all over before I realized. We had our first interchange of shots with them late this afternoon. The Little One was riding from the front to the flank. Evidently he did not think he was in range—nor did any of us. All at once Idaho tossed up his rifle and let go without aiming—or so it seemed to me. The stock was not at his shoulder before the report came. About six seconds after the smoke had cleared away we could see the Little One begin to lean backward in the saddle, and Idaho said grimly, 'I guess I got *you*.' The Little One leaned farther and farther till suddenly his head dropped back between his shoulder-blades. He held to his pony's mane with both hands for a long time and then all at once went off feet first.   His legs bent under him like putty as his feet touched the ground.   The pony bolted.

"Just as soon as Idaho fired the others closed right up and began riding around us at top speed, firing as they went.   Their aim was bad as a rule, but one bullet came very close to me.   At about half-past five they drew off out of range again and we made camp right where we stood.   Estorijo and I are both sure that Idaho hit the Red One, but Idaho himself is doubtful, and Bunt did not see the shot.   I could swear that the Red One all but went off his pony.   However, he seems active enough now.

"Monday morning.—Still another night without attack.   I have not slept since Friday evening.   The strain is terrific.   At daybreak this morning, when one of our ponies snorted suddenly, I cried out at the top of my voice. I could no more have repressed it than I could have stopped my blood flowing; and for half an hour afterward I could feel my flesh crisping and pringling, and there was a sickening weakness at the pit of my stomach. At breakfast I had to force down my coffee. They are still in place, but now there are two on each side, two in the front, two in the rear. The killing of the Little One seems to have heartened us all wonderfully. I am sure we will get out—somehow. But oh! the suspense of it.

"Monday morning, nine-thirty.—Under way for over two hours. There is no new development. But Idaho has just said that they seem to be edging in. We hope to reach water to-day. Our supply is low, and the ponies are beginning to hang their heads. It promises to be a blazing hot day. There is alkali all to the west of us, and we just commence to see the rise of ground miles to the southward that Idaho says is the San Jacinto Mountains. Plenty of water there. The desert hereabout is vast and lonesome beyond words; leagues of sparse sage-brush, leagues of leper-white alkali, leagues of baking gray sand, empty, heat-ridden, the abomination of desolation; and always—in whichever direction I turn my eyes—always, in the midst of this pale-yellow blur, a single figure in the distance, blanketed, watchful, solitary, standing out sharp and distinct against the background of sage and sand.

"Monday, about eleven o'clock.—No change. The heat is appalling. There is just a——

"Later.—I was on the point of saying that there was just a mouthful of water left for each of us in our canteens when Estorijo and Idaho both at the same time cried out that they were moving in. It is true. They are within rifle range, but do not fire. We, as well, have decided to reserve our fire until something more positive happens.

"Noon.—The first shot—for to-day—from the Red One. We are halted. The shot struck low and to the left. We could see the sand spout up in a cloud just as though a bubble had burst on the surface of the ground.

"They have separated from each other, and the whole eight of them are now in a circle around us. Idaho believes the Red One fired as a signal. Estorijo is getting ready to take a shot at the One with the Feather. We have the ponies in a circle around us. It looks as if now at last this was the beginning of the real business.

Later, twelve-thirty-five.—Estorijo missed. Idaho will try with the Winchester as soon as the One with the Feather halts. He is galloping toward the Red One.

"All at once, about two o'clock, the fighting began. This is the first let-up. It is now—

God knows what time. They closed up suddenly and began galloping about us in a circle, firing all the time. They rode like madmen. I would not have believed that Indian ponies could run so quickly. What with their yelling and the incessant crack of their rifles and the thud of their ponies' feet our horses at first became very restless, and at last Idaho's mustang bolted clean away. We all stood to it as hard as we could. For about the first fifteen minutes it was hot work. The Spotted One is hit. We are certain of that much, though we do not know whose gun did the work. My poor old horse is bleeding dreadfully from the mouth. He has two bullets in the stomach, and I do not believe he can stand much longer. They have let up for the last few moments, but are still riding around us, their guns at 'ready.' Every now and then one of us fires, but the heat shimmer has come up over the ground since noon and the range is extraordinarily deceiving.

"Three-ten.—Estorijo's horse is down, shot clean through the head. Mine has gone long since. We have made a rampart of the bodies.

"Three-twenty.—They are at it again, tearing around us incredibly fast, every now and then narrowing the circle. The bullets are striking everywhere now. I have no rifle, do

what I can with my revolver, and try to watch
what is going on in front of me and warn the
others when they press in too close on my side."
[*Karslake nowhere accounts for the absence of his
carbine. That a U. S. trooper should be without
his gun while traversing a hostile country is a fact
difficult to account for.*]

"Three-thirty.—They have winged me—
through the shoulder. Not bad, but it is
bothersome. I sit up to fire, and Bunt gives
me his knee on which to rest my right arm.
When it hangs it is painful.

"Quarter to four.—It is horrible. Bunt is
dying. He cannot speak, the ball having gone
through the lower part of his face, but back,
near the neck. It happened through his trying
to catch his horse. The animal was struck in
the breast and tried to bolt. He reared up,
backing away, and as we had to keep him close
to us to serve as a bulwark Bunt followed him
out from the little circle that we formed, his
gun in one hand, his other gripping the bridle.
I suppose every one of the eight fired at him
simultaneously, and down he went. The pony
dragged him a little ways still clutching the
bridle, then fell itself, its whole weight rolling
on Bunt's chest. We have managed to get
him in and secure his rifle, but he will not live.
None of us knows him very well. He only

joined us about a week ago, but we all liked him from the start.   He never spoke of himself, so we cannot tell much about him.   Idaho says he has a wife in Torreon, but that he has not lived with her for two years; they did not get along well together, it seems.   This is the first violent death I have ever seen, and it astonishes me to note how *unimportant* it seems.   How little anybody cares—after all.   If I had been told of his death—the details of it, in a story or in the form of fiction—it is easily conceivable that it would have impressed me more with its importance than the actual scene has done. Possibly my mental vision is scaled to a larger field since Friday, and as the greater issues loom up one man more or less seems to be but a unit—more or less—in an eternal series.   When he was hit he swung back against the horse, still holding by the rein.   His feet slid from under him, and he cried out, 'My *God!*' just once.   We divided his cartridges between us and Idaho passed me his carbine.   The barrel was scorching hot.

"They have drawn off a little and for fifteen minutes, though they still circle us slowly, there has been no firing.   Forty cartridges left. Bunt's body (I think he is dead now) lies just back of me, and already the gnats—I can't speak of it."

[Karslake evidently made the next few entries at successive intervals of time, but neglected in his excitement to note the exact hour as above. We may gather that "They" made another attack and then repeated the assault so quickly that he had no chance to record it properly. I transcribe the entries in exactly the disjointed manner in which they occur in the original. The reference to the "fire" is unexplainable.]

"I shall do my best to set down exactly what happened and what I do and think, and what I see.

"The heat-shimmer spoiled my aim, but I am quite sure that either

"This last rush was the nearest. I had started to say that though the heat-shimmer was bad, either Estorijo or myself wounded one of their ponies. We saw him stumble.

"Another rush——

"Our ammunition

"Only a few cartridges left.

"The Red One like a whirlwind only fifty yards away

"We fire separately now as they sneak up under cover of our smoke.

"We put the fire out.   Estorijo——"   *[It is possible that Karslake had begun here to chronicle the death of the Mexican.]*

"I have killed the Spotted One.   Just as he

wheeled his horse I saw him in a line with the rifle-sights and let him have it squarely. It took him straight in the breast. I could *feel* that shot strike. He went down like a sack of lead weights. By God, it was superb!

"Later.—They have drawn off out of range again, and we are allowed a breathing-spell. Our ponies are either dead or dying, and we have dragged them around us to form a barricade. We lie on the ground behind the bodies and fire over them. There are twenty-seven cartridges left.

"It is now mid-afternoon. Our plan is to stand them off if we can till night and then to try an escape between them. But to what purpose? They would trail us so soon as it was light.

"We think now that they followed us without attacking for so long because they were waiting till the lay of the land suited them. They wanted—no doubt—an absolutely flat piece of country, with no depressions, no hills or stream-beds in which we could hide, but which should be high upon the edges, like an amphitheatre. They would get us in the centre and occupy the rim themselves. Roughly, this is the bit of desert which witnesses our 'last stand.' On three sides the ground swells a very little— the rise is not four feet. On the third side it is open, and so flat that even lying on the ground as we do we can see (leagues away) the San Jacinto hills—'from whence cometh no help.' It is all sand and sage, forever and forever. Even the sage is sparse—a bad place even for a coyote. The whole is flagellated with an intolerable heat and—now that the shooting is relaxed—oppressed with a benumbing, sodden silence—the silence of a primordial world. Such a silence as must have brooded over the Face of the Waters on the Eve of Creation— desolate, desolate, as though a colossal, invisible pillar—a pillar of the Infinitely Still, the pillar of Nirvana—rose forever into the empty blue, human life an atom of microscopic dust crushed under its basis, and at the summit God Himself. And I find time to ask myself why, at this of all moments of my tiny life-span, I am able to write as I do, registering impressions, keeping a finger upon the pulse of the spirit. But oh! if I had time now—time to write down the great thoughts that do throng the brain. They are there, I feel them, know them. No doubt the supreme exaltation of approaching death is the stimulus that one never experiences in the humdrum business of the day-to-day existence. Such mighty thoughts! Unintelligible, but if I had time I could spell them out, *and how I could write then!* I feel

Drawn by Frederic Remington   CAUGHT IN THE CIRCLE   *Courtesy of Collier's Weekly*

The last stand of three troopers and a scout overtaken by a band of hostile Indians

that the whole secret of Life is within my reach;
I can almost grasp it; I seem to feel that in just
another instant I can see it all plainly, as the
archangels see it all the time, as the great minds
of the world, the great philosophers, have seen
it once or twice, vaguely—a glimpse here and
there, after years of patient study.   Seeing
thus I should be the equal of the gods.   But it
is not meant to be.   There is a sacrilege in it.
I almost seem to understand why it is kept
from us.   But the very reason of this with-
holding is in itself a part of the secret.   If I
could only, only set it down !—for whose eyes?
Those of a wandering hawk?   God knows.
But never mind.   I should have spoken—
once; should have said the great Word for
which the World since the evening and the
morning of the First Day has listened.   God
knows.   God knows.   What a whirl is this?
Monstrous incongruity.   Philosophy and fighting troopers.   The Infinite and dead horses.
There's humour for you.   The Sublime takes
off its hat to the Ridiculous.   Send a cartridge
clashing into the breech and speculate about
the Absolute.   Keep one eye on your sights
and the other on Cosmos.   Blow the reek of
burned powder from before you so you may
look over the edge of the abyss of the Great
Primal Cause.   Duck to the whistle of a bullet

and commune with Schopenhauer. Perhaps I
am a little mad. Perhaps I am supremely
intelligent. But in either case I am not under-
standable to myself. How, then, be under-
standable to others? If these sheets of paper,
this incoherence, is ever read, the others will
understand it about as much as the investiga-
ting hawk. But none the less be it of record
that I, Karslake, saw. It reads like Revelations:
'I, John, saw.' It is just that. There is something apocalyptic in it all. I have seen a vision,
but cannot—there is the pitch of anguish in
the impotence—bear record. If time were
allowed to order and arrange the words of de--
scription, this exaltation of spirit, in that very
space of time, would relax, and the describer
lapse back to the level of the average again
before he could set down the things he saw,
the things he thought. The machinery of the
mind that could coin the great Word is auto-
matic, and the very force that brings the die
near the blank metal supplies the motor power
of the reaction before the impression is made
. . . I stopped for an instant, looking up
from the page, and at once the great vague
panorama faded. I lost it all. Cosmos has
dwindled again to an amphitheatre of sage and
sand, a vista of distant purple hills, the shimmer
of scorching alkali, and in the middle distance

there, those figures, blanketed, beaded, feathered, rifle in hand.

"But for a moment I stood on Patmos.

"The Ridiculous jostles the elbow of the Sublime and shoulders it from place as Idaho announces that he has found two more cartridges in Estorijo's pockets.

"They rushed again. Eight more cartridges gone. Twenty-one left. They rush in this manner—at first the circle, rapid beyond expression, one figure succeeding the other so swiftly that the dizzied vision loses count and instead of seven of them there appear to be seventy. Then suddenly, on some indistinguishable signal, they contract this circle, and through the jets of powder-smoke Idaho and I see them whirling past our rifle-sights not one hundred yards away. Then their fire suddenly slackens, the smoke drifts by, and we see them in the distance again, moving about us at a slow canter. Then the blessed breathing-spell, while we peer out to know if we have killed or not, and count our cartridges. We have laid the twenty-one loaded shells that remain in a row between us, and after our first glance outward to see if any of them are down, our next is inward at that ever-shrinking line of brass and lead. We do not talk much. This is the end. We know it now. All of a sudden the conviction that I am to die here has hardened within me. It is, all at once, absurd that I should ever have supposed that I was to reach La Paz, take the east-bound train and report at San Antonio. It seems to me that I *knew*, weeks ago, that our trip was to end thus. I knew it—somehow—in Sonora, while we were waiting orders, and I tell myself that if I had only stopped to really think of it I could have foreseen to-day's bloody business.

"Later.—The Red One got off his horse and bound up the creature's leg. One of us hit him, evidently. A little higher, it would have reached the heart. Our aim is ridiculously bad—the heat-shimmer——

"Later.—Idaho is wounded. This last time, for a moment, I was sure the end had come. They were within revolver range and we could feel the vibration of the ground under their ponies' hoofs. But suddenly they drew off. I have looked at my watch; it is four o'clock.

"Four o'clock.—Idaho's wound is bad—a long, raking furrow in the right forearm. I bind it up for him, but he is losing a great deal of blood and is very weak.

"They seem to know that we are only two by now, for with each rush they grow bolder. The slackening of our fire must tell them how scant is our ammunition.

"Later.—This last was magnificent. The Red One and one other with lines of blue paint across his cheek galloped right at us. Idaho had been lying with his head and shoulders propped against the neck of his dead pony. His eyes were shut, and I thought he had fainted. But as he heard them coming he struggled up, first to his knees and then to his feet—to his full height—dragging his revolver from his hip with his left hand. The whole right arm swung useless. He was so weak that he could only lift the revolver half way—could not get the muzzle up. But though it sagged and dropped in his grip, he *would* die fighting. When he fired the bullet threw up the sand not a yard from his feet, and then he fell on his face across the body of the horse. During the charge I fired as fast as I could, but evidently to no purpose. They must have thought that Idaho was dead, for as soon as they saw him getting to his feet they sheered their horses off and went by on either side of us. I have made Idaho comfortable. He is unconscious; have used the last of the water to give him a drink. He does not seem——

"They continue to circle us. Their fire is incessant, but very wild. So long as I keep my head down I am comparatively safe.

"Later.—I think Idaho is dying. It seems

he was hit a second time when he stood up to
fire.   Estorijo is still breathing; I thought him
dead long since.

"Four-ten.—Idaho gone.   Twelve cartridges
left.   Am all alone now.

"Four-twenty-five.—I   am   very   weak."
[*Karslake was evidently wounded sometime between ten and twenty-five minutes after four.   His
notes make no mention of the fact.*]   "Eight cartridges remain.   I   leave   my   library   to   my
brother, Walter Patterson Karslake; all my
personal   effects   to   my   parents,   except   the
picture of myself taken in Baltimore in 1897,
which I direct to be " [*the next lines are undecipherable*] "   .   .   .   at Washington, D. C., as
soon as possible.   I appoint as my literary

"Four forty-five.—Seven cartridges.   Very
weak and unable to move lower part of my
body.   Am in no pain.   They rode in very
close.   The Red One is—— An intolerable
thirst——

"I   appoint as my literary executor my
brother, Patterson Karslake.   The notes on
'Coronado in New Mexico' should be revised.

"My death occurred in western Arizona,
April 15th, at the hands of a roving band of
Hunt-in-the-Morning's bucks.   They have——

"Five o'clock.—The last cartridge gone.

"Estorijo still breathing.   I cover his face

with my hat. Their fire is incessant. Am much weaker. Convey news of death to Patterson Karslake, care of Corn Exchange Bank, New York City.

"Five-fifteen—about.—They have ceased firing, and draw together in a bunch. I have four cartridges left" [*see conflicting note dated five o'clock*], "but am extremely weak. Idaho was the best friend I had in all the Southwest. I wish it to be known that he was a generous, open-hearted fellow, a kindly man, clean of speech, and absolutely unselfish. He may be known as follows: Sandy beard, long sandy hair, scar on forehead, about six feet one inch in height. His real name is James Monroe Herndon; his profession that of government scout. Notify Mrs. Herndon, Trinidad, New Mexico.

"The writer is Arthur Staples Karslake, dark hair, height five feet eleven, body will be found near that of Herndon.

"Luis Estorijo, Mexican——

"Later.—Two more cartridges.

"Five-thirty.—Estorijo dead.

"It is half-past five in the afternoon of April fifteenth. They followed us from the eleventh —Friday—till to-day. It will

[*The MS. ends here.*]

TWO HEARTS THAT BEAT AS ONE

TWO HEARTS THAT BEAT AS ONE

WHICH I puts it up as how you ain't never heard about that time that Hardenberg and Strokher—the Englisher—had a friendly go with bare knuckles—ten rounds it was—all along o' a feemale woman?"

It is a small world and I had just found out that my friend, Bunt McBride—horse-wrangler, miner, faro-dealer and bone-gatherer—whose world was the plains and ranges of the Great Southwest, was known of the Three Black Crows, Hardenberg, Strokher and Ally Bazan, and had even foregathered with them on more than one of their ventures for Cyrus Ryder's Exploitation Agency—ventures that had nothing of the desert in them, but that involved the sea, and the schooner, and the taste of the great-lunged canorous trades.

"Ye ain't never crossed the trail o' that mournful history?"

I professed my ignorance and said:

"They fought?"

"Mister Man," returned Bunt soberly, as one broaching a subject not to be trifled with, "They sure did. Friendly-like, y'know—like as how two high-steppin', sassy gents figures out to settle any little strained relations— friendly-like but considerable keen."

He took a pinch of tobacco from his pouch and a bit of paper and rolled a cigarette in the twinkling of an eye, using only one hand, in true Mexican style.

"Now," he said, as he drew the first long puff to the very bottom of the leathern valves he calls his lungs. "Now, I'm a-goin' for to relate that same painful proceedin' to you, just so as you kin get a line on the consumin' and devourin' foolishness o' male humans when they's a woman in the wind. Woman," said Bunt, wagging his head thoughtfully at the water, "woman is a weather-breeder. Mister Dixon, they is three things I'm skeered of. The last two I don't just rightly call to mind at this moment, but the first is woman. When I meets up with a feemale woman on my trail, I sheers off some prompt, Mr. Dixon; I sheers off. An' Hardenberg," he added irrelevantly, "would a-took an' married this woman, so he would. Yes, an' Strokher would, too."

"Was there another man?" I asked.

"No," said Bunt. Then he began to chuckle behind his mustaches. "Yes, they was." He smote a thigh. "They sure was another man for fair. Well, now, Mr. Man, lemmee tell you the whole '*how*.'

"It began with me bein' took into a wild-eyed scheme that that maverick, Cy Ryder, had cooked up for the Three Crows. They was a row down Gortamalar way. Same gesabe named Palachi—Barreto Palachi—findin' times dull an' the boys some off their feed, ups an' says to hisself, 'Exercise is wot I needs. I will now take an' overthrow the blame Gover'ment.' Well, this same Palachi rounds up a bunch o' *insurrectos* an' begins pesterin' an' badgerin' an' hectorin' the Gover'ment: an' r'arin' round an' bellerin' an' makin' a procession of hisself, till he sure pervades the landscape; an' before you knows what, lo'n beholt, here's a reel live Revolution-Thing cayoodlin' in the scenery, an' the Gover'ment is plum bothered.

"They rounds up the gesabe at last at a place on the coast, but he escapes as easy as how-do-you-do. He can't, howsomever, git back to his *insurrectos;* the blame Gover'ment being in possession of all the trails leadin' into the hinterland; so says he, 'What for a game would it be for me to hyke up to 'Frisco an' git in touch with my financial backers an' conspirate to smuggle down a load o' arms?' Which the same he does, and there's where the Three Black Crows an' me begin to take a hand.

"Cy Ryder gives us the job o' taking the schooner down to a certain point on the Gorta-malar coast and there delivering to the agent o' the gazabo three thousand stand o' forty-eight Winchesters.

"When we gits this far into the game Ryder ups and says:

" 'Boys, here's where I cashes right in.   You sets right to me for the schooner and the cargo. But you goes to Palachi's agent over 'crost the bay for instructions and directions.'

" 'But,' says the Englisher, Strokher, 'this bettin' a blind play don't suit our hand.   Why not' says he, 'make right up to Mister Palachi hisself?'

" 'No,' says Ryder, 'No, boys.   Ye can't. The Signor is lying as low as a toad in a wheel-track these days, because o' the pryin' and meddlin' disposition o' the local authorities. No,' he says, 'ye must have your palaver with the agent which she is a woman,' an' thereon I groans low and despairin'.

"So soon as he mentions 'feemale' I *knowed* trouble was in the atmosphere.   An' right there is where I sure looses my presence o' mind.   What I should a-done was to say, 'Mister Ryder, Hardenberg and gents all:

You're good boys an' you drinks and deals fair,
an' I loves you all with a love that can never,
never die for the terms o' your natural lives,
an' may God have mercy on your souls; *but* I
ain't keepin' case on this 'ere game no longer.
Woman and me is mules an' music. We ain't
never made to ride in the same go-cart. Good-
by.' That-all is wot I should ha' said. But
I didn't. I walked right plum into the sloo,
like the mudhead that I was, an' got mired
for fair—jes as I might a-knowed I would.

"Well, Ryder gives us a address over across
the bay an' we fair hykes over there all along o'
as crool a rain as ever killed crops. We finds
the place after awhile, a lodgin'-house all lorn
and loony, set down all by itself in the
middle o' some real estate extension like a
tepee in a 'barren'—a crazy 'modern' house
all gimcrack and woodwork and frostin',
with never another place in so far as you could
hear a coyote yelp.

"Well, we bucks right up an' asks o' the party
at the door if the Signorita Esperanza Ulivarri—
that was who Ryder had told us to ask for—
might be concealed about the premises, an' we
shows Cy Ryder's note. The party that
opened the door was a Greaser, the worst
looking I ever clapped eyes on—looked like
the kind wot 'ud steal the coppers off his dead

grandmother's eyes. Anyhow, he says to come in, gruff-like, an' to wait, *poco tiempo.*

"Well, we waited *moucho tiempo—muy moucho,* all a-settin' on the edge of the sofy, with our hats on our knees, like philly-loo birds on a rail, and a-countin' of the patterns in the wall-paper to pass the time along. An' Hardenberg, who's got to do the talkin', gets the fidgets byne-by; and because he's only restin' the toes o' his feet on the floor, his knees begin jiggerin'; an' along o' watchin' him, *my* knees begin to go, an' then Strokher's and then Ally Bazan's. An' there we sat all in a row and jiggered an' jiggered. Great snakes, it makes me sick to the stummick to think o' the idjeets we were.

"Then after a long time we hears a rustle o' silk petticoats, an' we all grabs holt o' one another an' looks scared-like, out from under our eyebrows. An' then—then, Mister Man, they walks into that bunk-house parlour the loveliest-lookin' young feemale woman that ever wore hair.

"She was lovelier than Mary Anderson; she was lovelier than Lotta. She was tall, an' black-haired, and had a eye . . . well, I dunno; when she gave you the littlest flicker o' that same eye, you felt it was about time to take an' lie right down an' say, 'I would esteem it, ma'am, a sure smart favour if you was to take an' wipe your boots on my waistcoat, jus' so's you could hear my heart a-beatin'. That's the kind o' feemale woman *she* was.

"Well, when Hardenberg had caught his second wind, we begins to talk business.

"'An' you're to take a passenger back with you,' says Esperanza after awhile.

"'What for a passenger might it be?' says Hardenberg.

"She fished out her calling-card at that and tore it in two an' gave Hardenberg one-half.

."'It's the party,' she says, 'that'll come aboard off San Diego on your way down an' who will show up the other half o' the card— the half I have here an' which the same I'm goin' to mail to him. An' you be sure the halves fit before you let him come aboard. An' when that party comes aboard,' she says, 'he's to take over charge.'

"'Very good,' says Hardenberg, mincing an' silly like a chessy cat lappin' cream. 'Very good, ma'am; your orders shall be obeyed.' He sure said it just like that, as if he spoke out o' a story-book. An' I kicked him under the table for it.

"Then we palavers a whole lot an' settles the way the thing is to be run, an' fin'ly, when

we'd got as far as could be that day, the
Signorita stood up an' says:

" 'Now me good fellows.' 'Twas Spanish she
spoke. 'Now, me good fellows, you must
drink a drink with me.' She herds us all up
into the dining-room and fetches out—not
whisky, mind you—but a great, fat, green-and-
gold bottle o' champagne, an' when Ally
Bazan has fired it off, she fills our glasses—
dinky little flat glasses that looked like flower
vases. Then she stands up there before us,
fine an' tall, all in black silk, an' puts her glass
up high an' sings out—

" 'To the Revolution!'

"An' we all solemn-like says, 'To the Revolution,' an' crooks our elbows. When we-all
comes to, about half an hour later, we're in
the street outside, havin' jus' said good-by to
the Signorita. We-all are some quiet the
first block or so, and then Hardenberg says—
stoppin' dead in his tracks:

" 'I pauses to remark that when a certain
young feemale party havin' black hair an' a
killin' eye gets good an' ready to travel up
the centre aisle of a church, I know the gent
to show her the way, which he is six feet one
in his stocking-feet, some freckled across the
nose, an' shoots with both hands.'

" 'Which the same observations,' speaks up

Strokher, twirlin' his yeller lady-killer, 'which
the same observations,' he says, 'has my hearty
indorsement an' coöperation savin' in the
particular of the description o' the gent. The
gent is five foot eleven high, three feet thick,
is the only son of my mother, an' has yeller
mustaches and a buck tooth.'

"'He don't qualify,' puts in Hardenberg.
'First, because he's a Englisher, and second,
because he's up again a American—and
besides, he has a tooth that's bucked.'

"'Buck or no buck,' flares out Strokher,
'wot might be the meanin' o' that remark
consernin' being a Englisher?'

"'The fact o' his bein' English,' says Hardenberg, 'is only half the hoe-handle. 'Tother
half being the fact that the first-named gent
is all American. No Yank ain't never took
no dust from aft a Englisher, whether it were
war, walkin'-matches, or women.'

"'But they's a Englisher,' sings out Strokher, 'not forty miles from here as can nick
the nose o' a freckled Yank if so be occasion
require.'

"Now ain't that plum foolish-like," observed Bunt, philosophically. "Ain't it plum
foolish-like o' them two gesabes to go flyin'
up in the air like two he-hens on a hot plate—
for nothin' in the world but because a neat

lookin' feemale woman has looked at 'em some soft?

"Well, naturally, we others—Ally Bazan an' me—we others throws it into 'em pretty strong about bein' more kinds of blame fools than a pup with a bug; an' they simmers down some, but along o' the way home I kin see as how they're a-glarin' at each other, an' a-drawin' theirselves up proud-like an' presumptchoous, an' I groans again, not loud but deep, as the Good Book says.

"We has two or three more palavers with the Signorita Esperanza and stacks the deck to beat the harbor police and the Customs people an' all, an' to nip down the coast with our contraband. An' each time we chins with the Signorita there's them two locoes steppin' and sidle'n' around her, actin' that silly-like that me and Ally Bazan takes an' beats our heads agin' the walls so soon as we're alone just because we're that pizen mortified.

"Fin'ly comes the last talky-talk an' we're to sail away next day an' mebbee snatch the little Joker through or be took an' hung by the *Costa Guardas*.

"An' 'Good-by,' says Hardenberg to Esperanza, in a faintin', die-away voice like a kitten with a cold. 'An' ain't we goin' to meet no more?'

" 'I sure hopes as much,' puts in Strokher, smirkin' so's you'd think he was a he-milliner sellin' a bonnet. 'I hope,' says he, 'our delightful acquaintanceship ain't a-goin' for to end abrupt this-a-way.'

" ' Oh, you nice, big Mister Men,' pipes up the Signorita in English, 'we will meet down there in Gortamalar soon again, yes, because I go down by the vapour carriages to-morrow.'

" ' Unprotected, too,' says Hardenberg, waggin' his fool head. 'An' so young !'

" Holy Geronimo ! I don't know what more fool drivelin' they had, but they fin'ly comes away. Ally Bazan and me rounds 'em up and conducts 'em to the boat an' puts 'em to bed like as if they was little—or drunk, an' the next day—or next night, rather—about one o'clock, we slips the heel ropes and hobbles o' the schooner quiet as a mountain-lion stalking a buck, and catches the out-tide through the gate o' the bay. Lord, we was some keyed up, lemmee tell you, an' Ally Bazan and Hardenberg was at the fore end o' the boat with their guns ready in case o' bein' asked impert'nent questions by the patrol-boats.

" Well, how-some-ever, we nips out with the little Jokers (they was writ in the manifest as minin' pumps) an' starts south. This 'ere

pasear down to Gortamalar is the first time I
goes a-gallying about on what the Three Crows
calls 'blue water'; and when that schooner hit
the bar I begins to remember that my stummick and inside arrangements ain't made o'
no chilled steel, nor yet o' rawhide. First I
gits plum sad, and shivery, and I feels as
mean an' pore as a prairie-dog w'ich 'as eat a
horned toad back'ards. I goes to Ally Bazan
and gives it out as how I'm going for to die, an'
I puts it up that I'm sure sad and depressed-
like; an' don't care much about life nohow;
an' that present surroundin's lack that certain
undescribable charm. I tells him that I
knows the ship is goin' to sink afore we git over
the bar. Waves!—they was higher'n the masts;
and I've rode some fair lively sun-fishers in
my time, but I ain't never struck anythin'
like the r'arin' and buckin' and high-an'-lofty
tumblin' that that same boat went through
with those first few hours after we had come
out.

"But Ally Bazan tells me to go downstairs
in the boat an' lie up quiet, an' byne-by I do
feel better. By next day I kin sit up and
take solid food again. An' then's when I
takes special notice o' the everlastin' foolishness o' Strokner and Hardenberg.

"You'd a thought each one o' them two

mush-heads was tryin' to act the part of a
ole cow which has had her calf took. They
goes a-moonin' about the boat that mournful
it 'ud make you yell jus' out o' sheer nervousness. First one 'ud up an' hold his head on
his hand an' lean on the fence-rail that ran
around the boat, and sigh till he'd raise his
pants clean outa the top o' his boots. An'
then the other 'ud go off in another part o' the
boat an' *he'd* sigh an' moon an' take on fit to
sicken a coyote.

"But byne-by—we're mebbee six days to
the good o' 'Frisco—byne-by they two gits
kind o' sassy along o' each t'other, an' they
has a heart-to-heart talk and puts it up as how
either one o' 'em 'ud stand to win so only the
t'other was out o' the game.

" 'It's double or nothing,' says Hardenberg,
who is somethin' o' a card sharp, 'for either
you or me, Stroke; an' if you're agreeable I'll
play you a round o' jacks for the chance at the
Signorita—the loser to pull out o' the running
for good an' all.'

"No, Strokher don't come in on no such
game, he says. He wins her, he says, as a man,
and not as no poker player. No, nor he won't
throw no dice for the chance o' winnin' Esperanza, nor he won't flip no coin, nor yet 'rastle.
'But,' says he all of a sudden, 'I'll tell you

which I'll do. You're a big, thick, strappin' hulk o' a two-fisted dray-horse, Hardie, an' I ain't no effete an' digenerate one-lunger myself. Here's wot I propose—that we-all takes an' lays out a sixteen-foot ring on the quarter-deck, an' that the raw-boned Yank and the stodgy Englisher strips to the waist, an' all-friendly-like, settles the question by Queens-bury rules an' may the best man win.'

"Hardenberg looks him over.

"'An' wot might be your weight?' says he. 'I don't figure on hurtin' of you, if so be you're below my class.'

"'I fights at a hunder and seventy,' says Strokher.

"'An' me,' says Hardenberg, 'at a hunder an' seventy-five. We're matched.'

"'Is it a go?' inquires Strokher.

"'You bet your great-gran'mammy's tortis-shell chessy cat it's a go,' says Hardenberg, prompt as a hop-frog catching flies.

"We don't lose no time trying to reason with 'em, for they is sure keen on havin' the go. So we lays out a ring by the rear end o' the deck, an' runs the schooner in till we're in the lee o' the land, an' she ridin' steady on her pins.

"Then along o' about four o'clock on a fine still day we lays the boat to, as they say, an'

folds up the sail, an' havin' scattered resin in
the ring (which it ain't no ring, but a square o'
ropes on posts), we says all is ready.

"Ally Bazan, he's referee, an' me, I'm the
time-keeper which I has to ring the ship's bell
every three minutes to let 'em know to quit
an' that the round is over.

"We gets 'em into the ring, each in his own
corner, squattin' on a bucket, the time-keeper
bein' second to Hardenberg an' the referee
being second to Strokher. An' then, after
they has shuk hands, I climbs up on' the
chicken-coop an' hollers 'Time' an' they begins.

"Mister Man, I've saw Tim Henan at his
best, an' I've saw Sayres when he was a top-
notcher, an' likewise several other irregler
boxin' sharps that were sure tough tarriers.
Also I've saw two short-horn bulls arguin'
about a question o' leadership, but so help me
Bob—the fight I saw that day made the others
look like a young ladies' quadrille. Oh, I ain't
goin' to tell o' that mill in detail, nor by rounds.
Rounds! After the first five minutes they
wa'n't no rounds. I rung the blame bell till I
rung her loose an' Ally Bazan yells 'break-a-
way' an' 'time's up' till he's black in the face,
but you could no more separate them two
than you could put the brakes on a blame
earthquake.

"At about suppertime we pulled 'em apart. We could do it by then, they was both so gone; an' jammed each one o' 'em down in their corners. I rings my bell good an' plenty, an' Ally Bazan stands up on a bucket in the middle o' the ring an' says:

"'I declare this 'ere glove contest a draw.'

"An' draw it sure was. They fit for two hours stiddy an' never a one got no better o' the other. They give each other lick for lick as fast an' as steady as they could stand to it. 'Rastlin', borin' in, boxin'—all was alike. The one was just as good as t'other. An' both willin' to the very last.

"When Ally Bazan calls it a draw, they gits up and wobbles toward each other an' shakes hands, and Hardenberg he says:

"'Stroke, I thanks you a whole lot for as neat a go as ever I mixed in.'

"An' Strokher answers up:

"'Hardie, I loves you better'n ever. You'se the first man I've met up with which I couldn't do for—an' I've met up with some scraggy propositions in my time, too.'

"Well, they two is a sorry-lookin' pair o' birds by the time we runs into San Diego harbour next night. They was fine lookin' objects for fair, all bruises and bumps. You remember now we was to take on a party at San Diego who was to show t'other half o' Esperanza's card, an' thereafterward to boss the job.

"Well, we waits till nightfall an' then slides in an' lays to off a certain pile o' stone, an' shows two green lights and one white every three and a half minutes for half a hour—this being a signal.

"They is a moon, an' we kin see pretty well. After we'd signaled about a hour, mebbee, we gits the answer—a one-minute green flare, and thereafterward we makes out a rowboat putting out and comin' towards us. They is two people in the boat. One is the gesabe at the oars an' the other a party sitting in the hinder end.

"Ally Bazan an' me, an' Strokher an' Hardenberg, we's all leanin' over the fence a-watchin'; when all to once I ups an' groans some sad. The party in the hinder end o' the boat bein' feemale.

"'Ain't we never goin' to git shut of 'em?' says I; but the words ain't no more'n off my teeth when Strokher pipes up:

"'It's *she*,' says he, gaspin' as though shot hard.

"'Wot!' cries Hardenberg, sort of mystified, 'Oh, I'm sure a-dreamin'!' he says, just that silly-like.

"'An' the mugs we've got!' says Strokher.

An' they both sets to swearin' and cussin' to beat all I ever heard.

"'I can't let her see me so bunged up,' says Hardenberg, doleful-like, 'Oh, whatever is to be done?'

"'An' *I* look like a real genuine blown-in-the-bottle pug,' whimpers Strokher. 'Never mind,' says he, 'we must face the music. We'll tell her these are sure honourable scars, got because we fit for her.'

"Well, the boat comes up an' the feemale party jumps out and comes up the let-down stairway, onto the deck. Without sayin' a word she hands Hardenberg the half o' the card and he fishes out his half an' matches the two by the light o' a lantern.

"By this time the rowboat has gone a little ways off, an' then at last Hardenberg says:

"'Welkum aboard, Signorita.'

"And Strokher cuts in with—

"'We thought it was to be a man that 'ud join us here to take command, but *you*,' he says—an' oh, butter wouldn't a-melted in his mouth—'But *you* he says, 'is always our mistress.

"'Very right, *bueno*. Me good fellows,' says the Signorita, 'but don't you be afraid that they's no man is at the head o' this business.' An' with that the party chucks

off hat an' skirts, *and I'll be Mexican if it
wa'n't a man after all!*

"'I'm the Signor Barreto Palachi, gentlemen,' says he. 'The gringo police who wanted
for to arrest me made the disguise necessary.
Gentlemen, I regret to have been obliged to
deceive such gallant *compadres;* but war knows
no law.'

"Hardenberg and Strokher gives one look
at the Signor and another at their own
spiled faces, then:

"'Come back here with the boat!' roars
Hardenberg over the side, and with that—
(upon me word you'd a-thought they two both
were moved with the same spring)—over they
goes into the water and strikes out hands over
hands for the boat as hard as ever they kin lay
to it. The boat meets 'em—Lord knows what
the party at the oars thought—they climbs in
an' the last I sees of 'em they was puttin' for
shore—each havin' taken a oar from the boat-
man, an' they sure was makin' that boat *hum.*

"Well, we sails away eventually without
'em; an' a year or more afterward I crosses
their trail again in Cy Ryder's office in
'Frisco.''

"Did you ask them about it all?" said I.

"Mister Man," observed Bunt. "I'm several
kinds of a fool; I know it. But sometimes

I'm wise.   I wishes for to live as long as I can,
an' die when I can't help it.   I does *not*, neither
there, nor thereafterward, ever make no joke,
nor yet no alloosion about, or concerning the
Signorita Esperanza Palachi in the hearin' o'
Hardenberg an' Strokher.   I've seen—(ye remember)—both those boys use their fists—
an' likewise Hardenberg, as he says hisself,
shoots with both hands."

THE DUAL PERSONALITY OF
SLICK DICK NICKERSON

THE DUAL PERSONALITY OF SLICK DICK NICKERSON

I

O N a certain morning in the spring of the year, the three men who were known as the Three Black Crows called at the office of "The President of the Pacific and Oriental Flotation Company," situated in an obscure street near San Francisco's water-front. They were Strokher, the tall, blond, solemn, silent Englishman; Hardenberg, the American, dry of humour, shrewd, resourceful, who bargained like a Vermonter and sailed a schooner like a Gloucester cod-fisher; and in their company, as ever inseparable from the other two, came the little colonial, nicknamed, for occult reasons, "Ally Bazan," a small, wiry man, excitable, vociferous, who was without fear, without guile and without money.

When Hardenberg, who was always spokesman for the Three Crows, had sent in their names, they were admitted at once to the inner office of the "President." The President was an old man, bearded like a prophet, with a watery blue eye and a forehead wrinkled like an orang's. He spoke to the Three Crows in the manner of one speaking to friends he has not seen in some time.

"Well, Mr. Ryder," began Hardenberg. "We called around to see if you had anything fer us this morning. I don't mind telling you that we're at liberty jus' now. Anything doing?"

Ryder fingered his beard distressfully. "Very little, Joe; very little."

"Got any wrecks?"

"Not a wreck."

Hardenberg turned to a great map that hung on the wall by Ryder's desk. It was marked in places by red crosses, against which were written certain numbers and letters. Hardenberg put his finger on a small island south of the Marquesas group and demanded: "What might be H. 33, Mr. President?"

"Pearl Island," answered the President. "Davidson is on that job."

"Or H. 125?" Hardenberg indicated a point in the Gilbert group.

"Guano deposits. That's promised."

"Hallo! You're up in the Aleutians. I make out. 20 A.—what's that?"

"Old government telegraph wire—line abandoned—finest drawn-copper wire. I've had three boys at that for months."

"What's 301? This here, off the Mexican coast?"

The President, unable to remember, turned to his one clerk: "Hyers, what's 301? Isn't that Peterson?"

The clerk ran his finger down a column: "No, sir; 301 is the Whisky Ship."

"Ah! So it is. I remember. *You* remember, too, Joe. Little schooner, the *Tropic Bird*—sixty days out from Callao—five hundred cases of whisky aboard—sunk in squall. It was thirty years ago. Think of five hundred cases of thirty-year-old whisky! There's money in that if I can lay my hands on the schooner. Suppose you try that, you boys—on a twenty per cent. basis. Come now, what do you say?"

"Not for *five* per cent.," declared Hardenberg. "How'd we raise her? How'd we know how deep she lies? Not for Joe. What's the matter with landing arms down here in Central America for Bocas and his gang?"

"I'm out o' that, Joe. Too much competition."

"What's doing here in Tahiti—No. 88? It ain't lettered."

Once more the President consulted his books.

"Ah!—88. Here we are. Cache o' illicit pearls. I had it looked up. Nothing in it."

"Say, Cap'n!"—Hardenberg's eye had traveled to the upper edge of the map— "whatever did you strike up here in Alaska? At Point Barrow, s'elp me Bob! It's 48 B."

The President stirred uneasily in his place. "Well, I ain't quite worked that scheme out, Joe. But I smell the deal. There's a Russian post along there some'eres. Where they catch sea-otters. And the skins o' sea-otters are selling this very day for seventy dollars at any port in China."

"I s'y," piped up Ally Bazan, "I knows a bit about that gyme. They's a bally kind o' Lum-tums among them Chinese as sports those syme skins on their bally clothes—as a mark o' rank, d'ye see."

"Have you figured at all on the proposition, Cap'n?" inquired Hardenberg.

"There's risk in it, Joe; big risk," declared the President nervously. "But I'd only ask fifteen per cent."

"You *have* worked out the scheme, then."

"Well—ah—y'see, there's the risk, and—ah——" Suddenly Ryder leaned forward, his watery blue eyes glinting: "Boys, it's a *jewel*. It's just your kind. I'd a-sent for you, to try on this very scheme, if you hadn't

shown up. You kin have the *Bertha Millner*—
I've a year's charter o' her from Wilbur—and
I'll only ask you fifteen per cent. of the *net*
profits—*net*, mind you."

"I ain't buyin' no dead horse, Cap'n,"
returned Hardenberg, "but I'll say this: we
pay no fifteen per cent."

"Banks and the Ruggles were daft to try it
and give me twenty-five."

"An' where would Banks land the scheme?
I know him. You put him on that German
cipher-code job down Honolulu way, an' it
cost you about a thousand before you
could pull out. We'll give you seven an' a
half."

"Ten," declared Ryder, "ten, Joe, at the
very least. Why, how much do you suppose
just the stores would cost me? And Point
Barrow—why, Joe, that's right up in the
Arctic. I got to run the risk o' you getting
the *Bertha* smashed in the ice."

"What do *we* risk?" retorted Hardenberg;
and it was the monosyllabic Strokher who gave
the answer:

"Chokee, by Jove!"

"Ten is fair. It's ten or nothing," answered
Hardenberg.

"Gross, then, Joe. Ten on the gross—or
I give the job to the Ruggles and Banks."

"Who's your bloomin' agent?" put in Ally Bazan.

"Nickerson. I sent him with Peterson on that *Mary Archer* wreck scheme. An' you know what Peterson says of him—didn't give him no trouble at all. One o' my best men, boys."

"There have been," observed Strokher stolidly, "certain stories told about Nickerson. Not that *I* wish to seem suspicious, but I put it to you as man to man."

"Ay," exclaimed Ally Bazan. "He was fair nutty once, they tell me. Threw some kind o' bally fit an' come aout all skew-jee'd in his mind. Forgot his nyme an' all. I s'y, how abaout him, anyw'y?"

"Boys," said Ryder, "I'll tell you. Nickerson—yes, I know the yarns about him. It was this way—y'see, I ain't keeping anything from you, boys. Two years ago he was a Methody preacher in Santa Clara. Well, he was what they call a revivalist, and he was holding forth one blazin' hot day out in the sun when all to once he goes down, *flat*, an' don't come round for the better part o' two days. When he wakes up he's *another person;* he'd forgot his name, forgot his job, forgot the whole blamed shooting-match. *And he ain't never remembered them since.* The doctors have names

for that kind o' thing. It seems it does happen
now and again. Well, he turned to an' began
sailoring first off—soon as the hospitals and
medicos were done with him—an' him not
having any friends as you might say, he was
let go his own gait. He got to be third mate
of some kind o' dough-dish down Mexico way;
and then I got hold o' him an' took him into
the Comp'ny. He's been with me ever since.
He ain't got the faintest kind o' recollection o'
his Methody days, an' believes he's always
been a sailorman. Well, that's *his* business,
ain't it? If he takes my orders an' walks
chalk, what do I care about his Methody game?
There, boys, is the origin, history and development of Slick Dick Nickerson. If you take up
this sea-otter deal and go to Point Barrow,
naturally Nick has got to go as owner's agent
and representative of the Comp'ny. But I
couldn't send a easier fellow to get along with.
Honest, now, I couldn't. Boys, you think
over the proposition between now and to-
morrow an' then come around and let me
know."

And the upshot of the whole matter was that
one month later the *Bertha Millner*, with
Nickerson, Hardenberg, Strokher and Ally
Bazan on board, cleared from San Francisco,
bound—the papers were beautifully precise—

for Seattle and Tacoma with a cargo of general merchandise.

As a matter of fact, the bulk of her cargo consisted of some odd hundreds of very fine lumps of rock—which as ballast is cheap by the ton—and some odd dozen cases of conspicuously labeled champagne.

The Pacific and Oriental Flotation Company made this champagne out of Rhine wine, effervescent salts, raisins, rock candy and alcohol. It was from the same stock of wine of which Ryder had sold some thousand cases to the Coreans the year before.

II

"NOT that I care a curse," said Strokher, the Englishman. "But I put it to you squarely that this voyage lacks that certain indescribable charm."

The *Bertha Millner* was a fortnight out, and the four adventurers—or, rather, the three adventurers and Nickerson—were lame in every joint, red-eyed from lack of sleep, half-starved, wholly wet and unequivocally disgusted. They had had heavy weather from the day they bade farewell to the whistling buoy off San Francisco Bay until the moment when even patient, docile, taciturn Strokher had at last—in his own fashion—rebelled.

"Ain't I a dam' fool? Ain't I a proper lot? Gard strike me if I don't chuck fer fair after this. Wot'd I come to sea fer—an' this 'ere go is the worst I *ever* knew—a baoat no bigger'n a bally bath-tub, head seas, livin' gyles the clock 'round, wet food, wet clothes, wet bunks. Caold till, by cricky! I've lost the feel o' mee feet. An' wat for? For the bloomin' good chanst o' a slug in mee guts. That's wat for."

At little intervals the little vociferous
colonial, Ally Bazan—he was red-haired and
speckled—capered with rage, shaking his fists.

But Hardenberg only shifted his cigar to
the other corner of his mouth. He knew Ally
Bazan, and knew that the little fellow would
have jeered at the offer of a first-cabin passage
back to San Francisco in the swiftest, surest,
steadiest passenger steamer that ever wore
paint. So he remarked: "I ain't ever billed
this promenade as a Coney Island picnic, I
guess."

Nickerson—Slick Dick, the supercargo—
was all that Hardenberg, who captained the
schooner, could expect. He never interfered,
never questioned; never protested in the name
or interests of the Company when Hardenberg
"hung on" in the bleak, bitter squalls till the
Bertha was rail under and the sails hard as
iron.

If it was true that he had once been a Methody
revivalist no one, to quote Alla Bazan, "could
a' smelled it off'n him." He was a black-
bearded, scrawling six-footer, with a voice like
a steam siren and a fist like a sledge. He
carried two revolvers, spoke of the Russians at
Point Barrow as the "Boomskys," and boasted
if it came to *that* he'd engage to account for
two of them, would shove their heads into their

boot-legs and give them the running scrag,
by God so he would!

Slowly, laboriously, beset in blinding fogs,
swept with icy rains, buffeted and mauled and
man-handled by the unending assaults of the
sea, the *Bertha Millner* worked her way northward up that iron coast—till suddenly she
entered an elysium.

Overnight she seemed to have run into it:
it was a world of green, wooded islands, of
smooth channels, of warm and steady winds,
of cloudless skies. Coming on deck upon the
morning of the *Bertha's* first day in this new
region, Ally Bazan gazed open-mouthed. Then:
"I s'y!" he yelled. "Hey! By crickey!
Look!" He slapped his thighs. "S'trewth!
This is 'eavenly."

Strokher was smoking his pipe on the hatch
combings. "Rather," he observed. "An' I
put it to you—we've deserved it."

In the main, however, the northward flitting
was uneventful. Every fifth day Nickerson
got drunk—on the Company's Corean champagne. Now that the weather had sweetened,
the Three Black Crows had less to do in the
way of handling and nursing the schooner.
Their plans when the "Boomskys" should be
reached were rehearsed over and over again.
Then came spells of card and checker playing,

story-telling, or hours of silent inertia when,
man fashion, they brooded over pipes in a
patch of sun, somnolent, the mind empty of
all thought.

But at length the air took on a keener tang;
there was a bite to the breeze, the sun lost his
savour and the light of him lengthened till
Hardenberg could read off logarithms at ten
in the evening. Great-coats and sweaters
were had from the chests, and it was no man's
work to reef when the wind came down from
out the north.

Each day now the schooner was drawing
nearer the Arctic Circle. At length snow fell,
and two days later they saw their first iceberg.

Hardenberg worked out their position on
the chart and bore to the eastward till he made
out the Alaskan coast—a smudge on the
horizon. For another week he kept this in
sight, the schooner dodging the bergs that by
now drove by in squadrons, and even bumping
and butling through drift and slush ice.

Seals were plentiful, and Hardenberg and
Strokher promptly revived the quarrel of their
respective nations. Once even they slew a
mammoth bull walrus—astray from some
northern herd—and played poker for the tusks.
Then suddenly they pulled themselves sharply
together, and, as it were, stood "attention."

For more than a week the schooner, following the trend of the far-distant coast, had headed eastward, and now at length, looming out of the snow and out of the mist, a somber bulwark, black, vast, ominous, rose the scarps and crags of that which they came so far to see—Point Barrow.

Hardenberg rounded the point, ran in under the lee of the land and brought out the chart which Ryder had given him. Then he shortened sail and moved west again till Barrow was "hull down" behind him. To the north was the Arctic, treacherous, nursing hurricanes, ice-sheathed; but close aboard, not a quarter of a mile off his counter, stretched a gray and gloomy land, barren, bleak as a dead planet, inhospitable as the moon.

For three days they crawled along the edge keeping their glasses trained upon every bay, every inlet. Then at length, early one morning, Ally Bazan, who had been posted at the bows, came scrambling aft to Hardenberg at the wheel. He was gasping for breath in his excitement.

"Hi! There we are," he shouted. "O Lord! Oh, I s'y! Now we're in fer it. That's them! That's them! By the great jumpin' jimminy Christmas, that's them fer fair! Strike me blind for a bleedin' gutter-cat if it

eyent. O Lord! S'y, I gotta to get drunk.
S'y, what-all's the first jump in the bally game
now?"

"Well, the first thing, little man," observed
Hardenberg, "is for your mother's son to
hang the monkey onto the safety-valve. Keep
y'r steam and watch y'r uncle."

"Scrag the Boomskys," said Slick Dick
encouragingly.

Strokher pulled the left end of his viking
mustache with the fingers of his right hand.

"We must now talk," he said.

A last conference was held in the cabin, and
the various parts of the comedy rehearsed.
Also the three looked to their revolvers.

"Not that I expect a rupture of diplomatic
relations," commented Strokher; "but if
there's any shooting done, as between man
and man, I choose to do it."

"All understood, then?" asked Hardenberg,
looking from face to face. "There won't be
no chance to ask questions once we set foot
ashore."

The others nodded.

It was not difficult to get in with the seven
Russian sea-otter fishermen at the post. Certain of them spoke a macerated English, and
through these Hardenberg, Ally Bazan and
Nickerson—Strokher remained on board to

look after the schooner—told to the "Boom-skys" a lamentable tale of the reported wreck of a vessel, described by Hardenberg, with laborious precision, as a steam whaler from San Francisco—the *Tiber* by name, bark-rigged, seven hundred tons burden, Captain Henry Ward Beecher, mate Mr. James Boss Tweed. They, the visitors, were the officers of the relief-ship on the lookout for castaways and survivors.

But in the course of these preliminaries it became necessary to restrain Nickerson—not yet wholly recovered from a recent incursion into the store of Corean champagne. It presented itself to his consideration as facetious to indulge (when speaking to the Russians) in strange and elaborate distortions of speech.

"And she sunk-avitch in a hundred fathom o' water-owski."

"—All on board-erewski."

"—hell of dam' bad storm-onavna."

And he persisted in the idiocy till Hardenberg found an excuse for taking him aside and cursing him into a realization of his position.

In the end—inevitably—the schooner's company were invited to dine at the post.

It was a strange affair—a strange scene. The coast, flat, gray, dreary beyond all power of expression, lonesome as the interstellar

space, and quite as cold, and in all that limitless
vastness of the World's Edge, two specks—the
hut, its three windows streaming with light,
and the tiny schooner rocking in the offing.
Over all flared the pallid incandescence of the
auroras.

The Company drank steadily, and Strokher,
listening from the schooner's quarterdeck,
heard the shouting and the songs faintly above
the wash and lapping under the counter.
Two hours had passed since the moment he
guessed that the feast had been laid. A third
went by. He grew uneasy. There was no
cessation of the noise of carousing. He even
fancied he heard pistol shots. Then after a
long time the noise by degrees wore down; a
long silence followed. The hut seemed deserted; nothing stirred; another hour went by.

Then at length Strokher saw a figure emerge
from the door of the hut and come down to
the shore. It was Hardenberg. Strokher saw
him wave his arm slowly, now to the left, now
to the right, and he took down the wig-wag as
follows: "Stand—in—closer—we—have—the
—skins."

III

DURING the course of the next few days
Strokher heard the different versions of the
affair in the hut over and over again till he
knew its smallest details. He learned how the
"Boomskys" fell upon Ryder's champagne
like wolves upon a wounded buck, how they
drank it from "enameled-ware" coffee-cups,
from tin dippers, from the bottles themselves;
how at last they even dispensed with the
tedium of removing the corks and knocked off
the heads against the table-ledge and drank
from the splintered bottoms; how they quarreled over the lees and dregs, how ever and
always fresh supplies were forthcoming, and
how at last Hardenberg, Ally Bazan and Slick
Dick stood up from the table in the midst of
the seven inert bodies; how they ransacked the
place for the priceless furs; how they failed to
locate them; how the conviction grew that this
was the wrong place after all, and how at length
Hardenberg discovered the trap-door that
admitted to the cellar, where in the dim light
of the uplifted lanterns they saw, corded in

169

tiny bales and packages, the costliest furs known to commerce.

Ally Bazan had sobbed in his excitement over that vision and did not regain the power of articulate speech till the "loot" was safely stowed in the 'tween-decks and Hardenberg had given order to come about.

"Now," he had observed dryly, "now, lads, it's Hongkong—or bust."

The tackle had fouled aloft and the jib hung slatting over the sprit like a collapsed balloon.

"Cast off up there, Nick!" called Hardenberg from the wheel.

Nickerson swung himself into the rigging, crying out in a mincing voice as, holding to a rope's end, he swung around to face the receding hut: "By-bye-skevitch. We've had *such* a charming evening. *Do* hope-sky we'll be able to come again-off." And as he spoke the lurch of the *Bertha* twitched his grip from the rope. He fell some thirty feet to the deck, and his head carromed against an iron cleat with a resounding crack.

"Here's luck," observed Hardenberg, twelve hours later, when Slick Dick, sitting on the edge of his bunk, looked stolidly and with fishy eyes from face to face. "We wa'n't quite short-handed enough, it seems."

"Dotty for fair. Dotty for fair," exclaimed

Ally Bazan; "clean off 'is nut. I s'y, Dick-ol'-chap, wyke-up, naow. Buck up. Buck up. '.Ave a drink."

But Nickerson could only nod his head and murmur: "A few more—consequently—and a good light——" Then his voice died down to unintelligible murmurs.

"We'll have to call at Juneau," decided Hardenberg two days later. "I don't figure on navigating this 'ere bath-tub to no Hong-kong whatsoever, with three hands. We gotta pick up a couple o' A. B.'s in Juneau, if so be we can."

"How about the loot?" objected Strokher. "If one of those hands gets between decks he might smell—a sea-otter, now. I put it to you he might."

"My son," said Hardenberg, "I've handled A. B.'s before;" and that settled the question.

During the first part of the run down, Nickerson gloomed silently over the schooner, looking curiously about him, now at his comrades' faces, now at the tumbling gray-green seas, now—and this by the hour—at his own hands. He seemed perplexed, dazed, trying very hard to get his bearings. But by and by he appeared, little by little, to come to himself. One day he pointed to the rigging with an unsteady forefinger, then, laying the same finger doubtfully upon his lips, said to Strokher: "A ship?"

"Quite so, quite so, me boy."

"Yes," muttered Nickerson absently, "a ship—of course."

Hardenberg expected to make Juneau on a Thursday. Wednesday afternoon Slick Dick came to him. He seemed never more master of himself. "How did I come aboard?" he asked.

Hardenberg explained.

"What have we been doing?"

"Why, don't you remember?" continued Hardenberg. He outlined the voyage in detail. "Then you remember," he went on, "we got up there to Point Barrow and found where the Russian fellows had their post, where they caught sea-otters, and we went ashore and got 'em all full and lifted all the skins they had——"

"'Lifted'? You mean *stole* them."

"Come here," said the other. Encouraged by Nickerson's apparent convalescence, Hardenberg decided that the concrete evidence of things done would prove effective. He led him down into the 'tween-decks. "See now," he said. "See this packing-case"—he pried up a board—"see these 'ere skins. Take one in y'r hand. Remember how we found 'em all in the cellar and hyked 'em out while the beggars slept?"

"*Stole* them? You say we got—that is *you* did—got somebody intoxicated and stole their property, and now you are on your way to dispose of it."

"Oh, well, if you want to put it thataway. Sure we did."

"I understand—— Well—— Let's go back on deck. I want to think this out."

The *Bertha Millner* crept into the harbour of Juneau in a fog, with ships' bells tolling on every side, let go her anchor at last in desperation and lay up to wait for the lifting. When this came the Three Crows looked at one another wide-eyed. They made out the drenched town and the dripping hills behind it. The quays, the custom house, the one hotel, and the few ships in the harbour. There were a couple of whalers from 'Frisco, a white, showily painted passenger boat from the same port, a Norwegian bark, and a freighter from Seattle grimy with coal-dust. These, however, the *Bertha's* company ignored. Another boat claimed all their attention. In the fog they had let go not a pistol-shot from her anchorage. She lay practically beside them. She was the United States revenue cutter *Bear*.

"But so long as they can't *smell* sea-otter

skin," remarked Hardenberg, "I don't know that we're any the worse."

"All the syme," observed Ally Bazan, "I don't want to lose no bloomin' tyme a-pecking up aour bloomin' A. B.'s."

"I'll stay aboard and tend the baby," said Hardenberg with a wink. "You two move along ashore and get what you can—Scoovies for choice. Take Slick Dick with you. I reckon a change o' air might buck him up."

When the three had gone, Hardenberg, after writing up the painfully doctored log, set to work to finish a task on which the adventurers had been engaged in their leisure moments since leaving Point Barrow. This was the counting and sorting of the skins. The packing-case had been broken open, and the scanty but precious contents littered an improvised table in the hold. Pen in hand, Hardenberg counted and ciphered and counted again. He could not forbear a chuckle when the net result was reached. The lot of the skins—the pelt of the sea-otter is ridiculously small in proportion to its value—was no heavy load for the average man. But Hardenberg knew that once the "loot" was safely landed at the Hongkong pierhead the Three Crows would share between them close upon ten thousand dollars. Even— if they had luck, and could dispose of the skins singly or in small lots—that figure might be doubled.

"And I call it a neat turn," observed Hardenberg. He was aroused by the noise of hurried feet upon the deck, and there was that in their sound that brought him upright in a second, hand on hip. Then, after a second, he jumped out on deck to meet Ally Bazan and Strokher, who had just scrambled over the rail.

"Bust. B-u-s-t !" remarked the Englishman.

"'Ere's 'ell to pay," cried Ally Bazan in a hoarse whisper, glancing over at the revenue cutter.

"Where's Nickerson?" demanded Hardenberg.

"That's it," answered the colonial. "That's where it's 'ell. Listen naow. He goes ashore along o' us, quiet and peaceable like, never battin' a eye, we givin' him a bit o' jolly, y' know, to keep him chirked up as ye might s'y. But so soon as ever he sets foot on shore, abaout faice he gaoes, plumb into the Custom's orfice. I s'ys, 'Wot all naow, messmite? Come along aout o' that.' But he turns on me like a bloomin' babby an s'ys he : 'Hands orf, wretch !' Ay, them's just his words. Just like that, 'Hands orf, wretch !' And then he nips into the orfice an' marches fair up to the desk an' sy's like this—we heerd him, havin' followed on to the door—he s'ys, just like this:

" 'Orfficer, I am a min'ster o' the gospel, o' the Methodis' denomineye-tion, an' I'm deteyined agin my will along o' a pirate ship which has robbed certain parties o' val-able goods. Which syme I'm pre-pared to attest afore a no'try publick, an' lodge informeye-tion o' crime. An',' s'ys he, 'I demand the protection o' the authorities an' arsk to be directed to the American consul.'

"S'y, we never wyted to hear no more, but hyked awye hot foot. S'y, wot all now. Oh, mee Gord! eyen't it a rum gao for fair? S'y, let's get aout o' here, Hardy, dear."

"Look there," said Hardenberg, jerking his head toward the cutter, "how far'd' we get before the customs would 'a' passed the tip to *her* and she'd started to overhaul us? That's what they feed her for—to round up the likes o' us."

"We got to do something rather soon," put in Strokher. "Here comes the custom house dinghy now."

As a matter of fact, a boat was putting off from the dock. At her stern fluttered the custom house flag.

"Bitched—bitched for fair!" cried Ally Bazan.

From a drawing by Lucius Hitchcock

"'ERE'S 'ELL TO PAY!"

Courtesy of Collier's Weekly

"Quick, now!" exclaimed Hardenberg. "On the jump! Overboard with that loot!—or no. Steady! That won't do. There's that dam' cutter. They'd see it go. Here!—into the galley. There's a fire in the stove. Get a move on!"

"Wot!" wailed Ally Bazan. "Burn the little joker. Gord, I *can't*, Hardy, I *can't*. It's agin human nature."

"You can do time in San Quentin, then, for felony," retorted Strokher as he and Hardenberg dashed by him, their arms full of the skins. "You can do time in San Quentin else. Make your choice. I put it to you as between man and man."

With set teeth, and ever and again glancing over the rail at the oncoming boat, the two fed their fortune to the fire. The pelts, partially cured and still fatty, blazed like crude oil, the hair crisping, the hides melting into rivulets of grease. For a minute the schooner reeked of the smell and a stifling smoke poured from the galley stack. Then the embers of the fire guttered and a long whiff of sea wind blew away the reek. A single skin, fallen in the scramble, still remained on the floor of the galley. Hardenberg snatched it up, tossed it into the flames and clapped the door to. "Now, let him squeal," he declared. "You fellows, when that boat gets here, let *me* talk; keep your mouths shut or, by God, we'll all wear stripes."

The Three Crows watched the boat's approach in a silence broken only once by a long whimper from Ally Bazan. "An' it was a-workin' out as lovely as Billy-oh," he said, "till that syme underbred costermonger's swipe remembered he was Methody—an' him who, only a few d'ys back, went raound s'yin' 'scrag the "Boom-skys"!' A couple o' thousand pounds gone as quick as look at it. Oh, I eyn't never goin' to git over this."

The boat came up and the Three Crows were puzzled to note that no brass-buttoned person-age sat in the stern-sheets, no harbour police glowered at them from the bow, no officer of the law fixed them with the eye of suspicion. The boat was manned only by a couple of freight-handlers in woolen Jerseys, upon the breasts of which were affixed the two letters, "C. H "

"Say," called one of the freight-handlers, "is this the *Bertha Millner?*"

"Yes," answered Hardenberg, his voice at a growl. "An' what might you want with her, my friend?"

"Well, look here," said the other, "one of your hands came ashore mad as a coot and broke into the house of the American Consul, and resisted arrest and raised hell generally. The inspector says you got to send a provost guard or something ashore to take him off. There's been several mix-ups among ships' crews lately and the town——"

The tide drifted the boat out of hearing, and Hardenberg sat down on the capstan head, turning his back to his comrades. There was a long silence. Then he said:

" Boys, let's go home. I—I want to have a talk with President Ryder."

THE SHIP THAT SAW A GHOST

THE SHIP THAT SAW A GHOST

VERY much of this story must remain untold, for the reason that if it were definitely known what business I had aboard the tramp steam-freighter *Glarus*, three hundred miles off the South American coast on a certain summer's day, some few years ago, I would very likely be obliged to answer a great many personal and direct questions put by fussy and impertinent experts in maritime law—who are paid to be inquisitive. Also, I would get "Ally Bazan," Strokher and Hardenberg into trouble.

Suppose on that certain summer's day, you had asked of Lloyds' agency where the *Glarus* was, and what was her destination and cargo. You would have been told that she was twenty days out from Callao, bound north to San Francisco in ballast; that she had been spoken by the bark *Medea* and the steamer *Benevento;* that she was reported to have blown out a cylinder head, but being manageable was proceeding on her way under sail.

That is what Lloyds would have answered.

If you know something of the ways of ships and what is expected of them, you will under-

stand that the *Glarus*, to be some half a dozen
hundred miles south of where Lloyds' would
have her, and to be still going south, under full
steam, was a scandal that would have made
her brothers and sisters ostracize her finally
and forever.

And that is curious, too. Humans may
indulge in vagaries innumerable, and may go
far afield in the way of lying; but a ship may
not so much as quibble without suspicion.
The least lapse of "regularity," the least diffi-
culty in squaring performance with intuition,
and behold she is on the black list, and her
captain, owners, officers, agents and consignors,
and even supercargoes, are asked to explain.

And the *Glarus* was already on the black list.
From the beginning her stars had been malign.
As the *Breda*, she had first lost her reputation,
seduced into a filibustering escapade down the
South American coast, where in the end a plain-
clothes United States detective—that is to say,
a revenue cutter—arrested her off Buenos Ayres
and brought her home, a prodigal daughter,
besmirched and disgraced.

After that she was in some dreadful black-
birding business in a far quarter of the South
Pacific; and after that—her name changed
finally to the *Glarus*—poached seals for a
syndicate of Dutchmen who lived in Tacoma,

and who afterward built a club-house out of
what she earned.

And after that we got her.

We got her, I say, through Ryder's South
Pacific Exploitation Company. The "President" had picked out a lovely little deal for
Hardenberg, Strokher and Ally Bazan (the
Three Black Crows), which he swore would
make them "independent rich" the rest of their
respective lives. It is a promising deal (B. 300
it is on Ryder's map), and if you want to know
more about it you may write to ask Ryder
what B. 300 is. If he chooses to tell you, that
is his affair.

For B. 300—let us confess it—is, as Hardenberg puts it, as crooked as a dog's hind leg. It
is as risky as barratry. If you pull it off you
may—after paying Ryder his share—divide
sixty-five, or possibly sixty-seven, thousand
dollars between you and your associates. If
you fail, and you are perilously like to fail, you
will be sure to have a man or two of your com-
panions shot, maybe yourself obliged to pistol
certain people, and in the end fetch up at Tahiti,
prisoner in a French patrol-boat.

Observe that B. 300 is spoken of as still open.
It is so, for the reason that the Three Black
Crows did not pull it off. It still stands marked
up in red ink on the map that hangs over

Ryder's desk in the San Francisco office; and any one can have a chance at it who will meet Cyrus Ryder's terms. Only he can't get the *Glarus* for the attempt.

For the trip to the island after B. 300 was the last occasion on which the *Glarus* will smell blue water or taste the trades. She will never clear again. She is lumber.

And yet the *Glarus* on this very blessed day of 1902 is riding to her buoys off Sausalito in San Francisco Bay, complete in every detail (bar a broken propeller shaft), not a rope missing, not a screw loose, not a plank started— a perfectly equipped steam-freighter.

But you may go along the "Front" in San Francisco from Fisherman's Wharf to the China steamships' docks and shake your dollars under the seamen's noses, and if you so much as whisper *Glarus* they will edge suddenly off and look at you with scared suspicion, and then, as like as not, walk away without another word. No pilot will take the *Glarus* out; no captain will navigate her; no stoker will feed her fires; no sailor will walk her decks. The *Glarus* is suspect. She has seen a ghost.

.   .   .   .   .

It happened on our voyage to the island after this same B. 300. We had stood well off from shore for day after day, and Hardenberg had shaped our course so far from the track of navigation that since the *Benevento* had hulled down and vanished over the horizon no stitch of canvas nor smudge of smoke had we seen. We had passed the equator long since, and would fetch a long circuit to the southard, and bear up against the island by a circuitous route. This to avoid being spoken. It was tremendously essential that the *Glarus* should not be spoken.

I suppose, no doubt, that it was the knowledge of our isolation that impressed me with the dreadful remoteness of our position. Certainly the sea in itself looks no different at a thousand than at a hundred miles from shore. But as day after day I came out on deck at noon, after ascertaining our position on the chart (a mere pin-point in a reach of empty paper), the sight of the ocean weighed down upon me with an infinitely great awesomeness—and I was no new hand to the high seas even then.

But at such times the *Glarus* seemed to me to be threading a loneliness beyond all worlds and beyond all conception desolate. Even in more populous waters, when no sail notches the line of the horizon, the propinquity of one's kind is nevertheless a thing understood, and to an unappreciated degree comforting. Here, however, I knew we were out, far out in the desert. Never a keel for years upon years before us had parted these waters; never a sail had bellied to these winds. Perfunctorily, day in and day out we turned our eyes through long habit toward the horizon. But we knew, before the look, that the searching would be bootless. Forever and forever, under the pitiless sun and cold blue sky stretched the indigo of the ocean floor. The ether between the planets can be no less empty, no less void.

I never, till that moment, could have so much as conceived the imagination of such loneliness, such utter stagnant abomination of desolation. In an open boat, bereft of comrades, I should have gone mad in thirty minutes.

I remember to have approximated the impression of such empty immensity only once before, in my younger days, when I lay on my back on a treeless, bushless mountainside and stared up into the sky for the better part of an hour.

You probably know the trick. If you do not, you must understand that if you look up at the blue long enough, the flatness of the thing begins little by little to expand, to give here and there; and the eye travels on and on and up and up, till at length (well for you that it lasts but the fraction of a second), you all at once see space. You generally stop there and cry out, and—your hands over your eyes—are only too glad to grovel close to the good old solid earth again. Just as I, so often on short voyage, was glad to wrench my eyes away from that horrid vacancy, to fasten them upon our sailless masts and stack, or to lay my grip upon the sooty smudged taffrail of the only thing that stood between me and the Outer Dark.

For we had come at last to that region of the Great Seas where no ship goes, the silent sea of Coleridge and the Ancient One, the unplumbed, untracked, uncharted Dreadfulness, primordial, hushed, and we were as much alone as a grain of star-dust whirling in the empty space beyond Uranus and the ken of the greater telescopes.

So the *Glarus* plodded and churned her way onward. Every day and all day the same pale-blue sky and the unwinking sun bent over that moving speck. Every day and all day the same black-blue water-world, untouched by any known wind, smooth as a slab of syenite, colourful as an opal, stretched out and around and beyond and before and behind us, forever, illimitable, empty. Every day the smoke of our fires veiled the streaked whiteness of our wake. Every day Hardenberg (our skipper) at noon pricked a pin-hole in the chart that hung in the wheel-house, and that showed we were so much farther into the wilderness. Every day the world of men, of civilization, of newspapers, policemen and street-railways receded, and we steamed on alone, lost and forgotten in that silent sea.

"Jolly lot o' room to turn raound in," observed Ally Bazan, the colonial, "withaout steppin' on y'r neighbour's toes."

"We're clean, clean out o' the track o' navigation," Hardenberg told him. "An' a blessed good thing for us, too. Nobody ever comes down into these waters. Ye couldn't pick no course here. Everything leads to nowhere."

"Might as well be in a bally balloon," said Strokher.

I shall not tell of the nature of the venture on which the *Glarus* was bound, further than to say it was not legitimate. It had to do with an ill thing done more than two centuries ago. There was money in the venture, but it was not to be gained by a violation of metes and bounds which are better left intact.

The island toward which we were heading is associated in the minds of men with a Horror.

A ship had called there once, two hundred years in advance of the *Glarus*—a ship not much unlike the crank high-prowed caravel of Hudson, and her company had landed, and having accomplished the evil they had set out to do, made shift to sail away. And then, just after the palms of the island had sunk from sight below the water's edge, the unspeakable had happened. The Death that was not Death had arisen from out the sea and stood before the ship, and over it, and the blight of the thing lay along the decks like mould, and the ship sweated in the terror of that which is yet without a name.

Twenty men died in the first week, all but six in the second. These six, with the shadow of insanity upon them, made out to launch a boat, returned to the island and died there, after leaving a record of what had happened.

The six left the ship exactly as she was, sails all set, lanterns all lit—left her in the shadow of the Death that was not Death.

She stood there, becalmed, and watched them go. She was never heard of again.

Or was she—well, that's as may be.

But the main point of the whole affair, to my notion, has always been this. The ship was the last friend of those six poor wretches

who made back for the island with their poor
chests of plunder. She was their guardian,
as it were, would have defended and befriended
them to the last; and also we, the Three Black
Crows and myself, had no right under heaven,
nor before the law of men, to come prying and
peeping into this business—into this affair of
the dead and buried past. There was sacrilege
in it. We were no better than body-snatchers.

.   .   .   .   .   .

When I heard the others complaining of the
loneliness of our surroundings, I said nothing
at first. I was no sailor man, and I was on
board only by tolerance. But I looked again
at the maddening sameness of the horizon—
the same vacant, void horizon that we had
seen now for sixteen days on end, and felt in
my wits and in my nerves that same formless
rebellion and protest such as comes when the
same note is reiterated over and over again.

It may seem a little thing that the mere fact
of meeting with no other ship should have
ground down the edge of the spirit. But let
the incredulous—bound upon such a hazard
as ours—sail straight into nothingness for
sixteen days on end, seeing nothing but the
sun, hearing nothing but the thresh of his
own screw, and then put the question.

And yet, of all things, we desired no company.

Stealth was our one great aim. But I think there were moments—toward the last—when the Three Crows would have welcomed even a cruiser.

Besides, there was more cause for depression, after all, than mere isolation.

On the seventh day Hardenberg and I were forward by the cat-head, adjusting the grain with some half-formed intent of spearing the porpoises that of late had begun to appear under our bows, and Hardenberg had been computing the number of days we were yet to run.

"We are some five hundred odd miles off that island by now," he said, "and she's doing her thirteen knots handsome. All's well so far—but do you know, I'd just as soon raise that point o' land as soon as convenient."

"How so?" said I, bending on the line. "Expect some weather?"

"Mr. Dixon," said he, giving me a curious glance, "the sea is a queer proposition, put it any ways. I've been a seafarin' man since I was big as a minute, and I know the sea, and what's more, the Feel o' the sea. Now, look out yonder. Nothin', hey? Nothin' but the same ol' skyline we've watched all the way out. The glass is as steady as a steeple, and this ol' hooker, I reckon, is as sound as the

day she went off the ways. But just the same
if I were to home now, a-foolin' about Gloucester
way in my little dough-dish—d'ye know what?
I'd put into port. I sure would. Because
why? Because I got the Feel o' the Sea, Mr.
Dixon. I got the Feel o' the Sea."

I had heard old skippers say something of
this before, and I cited to Hardenberg the
experience of a skipper captain I once knew
who had turned turtle in a calm sea off Trincomalee. I ask him what this Feel of the Sea
was warning him against just now (for on the
high sea any premonition is a premonition of
evil, not of good). But he was not explicit.

"I don't know," he answered moodily,
and as if in great perplexity, coiling the rope
as he spoke. "I don't know. There's some
blame thing or other close to us, I'll bet a hat.
I don't know the name of it, but there's a
big Bird in the air, just out of sight som'eres,
and," he suddenly exclaimed, smacking his
knee and leaning forward, "I—don't—like—
it—one—dam'—bit."

The same thing came up in our talk in the
cabin that night, after the dinner was taken
off and we settled down to tobacco. Only,
at this time, Hardenberg was on duty on the
bridge. It was Ally Bazan who spoke instead.

"Seems to me," he hazarded, "as haow

they's somethin' or other a-goin' to bump up
pretty blyme soon. I shouldn't be surprised,
naow, y'know, if we piled her up on some bally
uncharted reef along o' to-night and went
strite daown afore we'd had a bloomin' charnce
to s'y 'So long, gen'lemen all.'"

He laughed as he spoke, but when, just at
that moment, a pan clattered in the galley,
he jumped suddenly with an oath, and looked
hard about the cabin.

Then Strokher confessed to a sense of distress also. He'd been having it since day
before yesterday, it seemed.

"And I put it to you the glass is
lovely," he said, "so it's no blow. I guess,"
he continued, "we're all a bit seedy and
ship-sore."

And whether or not this talk worked upon
my own nerves, or whether in very truth the
Feel of the Sea had found me also, I do not
know; but I do know that after dinner that
night, just before going to bed, a queer sense
of apprehension came upon me, and that when
I had come to my stateroom, after my turn
upon deck, I became furiously angry with
nobody in particular, because I could not at
once find the matches. But here was a difference. The other man had been merely vaguely
uncomfortable.

I could put a name to my uneasiness. I
felt that we were being watched.

. . . . . .

It was a strange ship's company we made
after that. I speak only of the Crows and
myself. We carried a scant crew of stokers,
and there was also a chief engineer. But we
saw so little of him that he did not count.
The Crows and I gloomed on the quarterdeck
from dawn to dark, silent, irritable, working
upon each other's nerves till the creak of a
block would make a man jump like cold steel
laid to his flesh. We quarreled over absolute
nothings, glowered at each other for half a
word, and each one of us, at different times,
was at some pains to declare that never in the
course of his career had he been associated
with such a disagreeable trio of brutes. Yet
we were always together, and sought each
other's company with painful insistence.

Only once were we all agreed, and that was
when the cook, a Chinaman, spoiled a certain
batch of biscuits. Unanimously we fell foul
of the creature with so much vociferation as
fishwives till he fled the cabin in actual fear
of mishandling, leaving us suddenly seized
with noisy hilarity—for the first time in a
week. Hardenberg proposed a round of drinks
from our single remaining case of beer. We

stood up and formed an Elk's chain and then drained our glasses to each other's health with profound seriousness.

That same evening, I remember, we all sat on the quarterdeck till late and—oddly enough —related each one his life's history up to date; and then went down to the cabin for a game of euchre before turning in.

We had left Strokher on the bridge—it was his watch—and had forgotten all about him in the interest of the game, when—I suppose it was about one in the morning—I heard him whistle long and shrill. I laid down my cards and said:

"Hark!"

In the silence that followed we heard at first only the muffled lope of our engines, the cadenced snorting of the exhaust, and the ticking of Hardenberg's big watch in his waistcoat that he had hung by the arm-hole to the back of his chair. Then from the bridge, above our deck, prolonged, intoned— a wailing cry in the night—came Strokher's voice:

"Sail oh-h-h."

And the cards fell from our hands, and, like men turned to stone, we sat looking at each other across the soiled red cloth for what seemed an immeasurably long minute.

Then stumbling and swearing, in a hysteria of hurry, we gained the deck.

There was a moon, very low and reddish, but no wind. The sea beyond the taffrail was as smooth as lava, and so still that the swells from the cutwater of the *Glarus* did not break as they rolled away from the bows.

I remember that I stood staring and blinking at the empty ocean—where the moonlight lay like a painted stripe reaching to the horizon —stupid and frowning, till Hardenberg, who had gone on ahead, cried:

"Not here—on the bridge!"

We joined Strokher, and as I came up the others were asking:

"Where? Where?"

And there, before he had pointed, I saw— we all of us saw—— And I heard Hardenberg's teeth come together like a spring trap, while Ally Bazan ducked as though to a blow, muttering:

"Gord 'a' mercy, what nyme do ye put to a ship like that?"

And after that no one spoke for a long minute, and we stood there, moveless black shadows, huddled together for the sake of the blessed elbow touch that means so incalculably much, looking off over our port quarter.

For the ship that we saw there—oh, she was

not a half-mile distant—was unlike any ship known to present day construction.

She was short, and high-pooped, and her stern, which was turned a little toward us, we could see, was set with curious windows, not unlike a house. And on either side of this stern were two great iron cressets such as once were used to burn signal-fires in. She had three masts with mighty yards swung 'thwart ship, but bare of all sails save a few rotting streamers. Here and there about her a tangled mass of rigging drooped and sagged.

And there she lay, in the red eye of the setting moon, in that solitary ocean, shadowy, antique, forlorn, a thing the most abandoned, the most sinister I ever remember to have seen.

Then Strokher began to explain volubly and with many repetitions.

"A derelict, of course. I was asleep; yes, I was asleep. Gross neglect of duty. I say I was asleep—on watch. And we worked up to her. When I woke, why—you see, when I woke, there she was," he gave a weak little laugh, "and—and now, why, there she is, you see. I turned around and saw her sudden like—when I woke up, that is."

He laughed again, and as he laughed the engines far below our feet gave a sudden hiccough. Something crashed and struck the

ship's sides till we lurched as we stood.
There was a shriek of steam, a shout—and
then silence.

The noise of the machinery ceased; the *Glarus*
slid through the still water, moving only by
her own decreasing momentum.

Hardenberg sang, "Stand by!" and called
down the tube to the engine-room.

"What's up?"

I was standing close enough to him to hear
the answer in a small, faint voice:

"Shaft gone, sir."

"Broke?"

"Yes, sir."

Hardenberg faced about.

"Come below. We must talk." I do not
think any of us cast a glance at the Other Ship
again. Certainly I kept my eyes away from
her. But as we started down the companionway I laid my hand on Strokher's shoulder.
The rest were ahead. I looked him straight
between the eyes as I asked:

"Were you asleep? Is that why you saw
her so suddenly?"

It is now five years since I asked the question. I am still waiting for Strokher's answer.

Well, our shaft was broken. That was flat.
We went down into the engine-room and saw
the jagged fracture that was the symbol of our

broken hopes. And in the course of the next
five minutes' conversation with the chief we
found that, as we had not provided against
such a contingency, there was to be no mending
of it. We said nothing about the mishap
coinciding with the appearance of the Other
Ship. But I know we did not consider the
break with any degree of surprise after a few
moments.

We came up from the engine-room and sat
down to the cabin table.

"Now what?" said Hardenberg, by way of
beginning.

Nobody answered at first.

It was by now three in the morning. I recall
it all perfectly. The ports opposite where I
sat were open and I could see. The moon was
all but full set. The dawn was coming up with
a copper murkiness over the edge of the world.
All the stars were yet out. The sea, for all
the red moon and copper dawn, was gray, and
there, less than half a mile away, still lay our
consort. I could see her through the portholes
with each slow careening of the *Glarus*.

"I vote for the island," cried Ally Bazan,
"shaft or no shaft. We rigs a bit o' syle,
y'know——" and thereat the discussion began.

For upward of two hours it raged, with loud
words and shaken forefingers, and great noisy

bangings of the table, and how it would have
ended I do not know, but at last—it was then
maybe five in the morning—the lookout passed
word down to the cabin:

"Will you come on deck, gentlemen?" It
was the mate who spoke, and the man was
shaken—I could see that—to the very vitals
of him. We started and stared at one another,
and I watched little Ally Bazan go slowly
white to the lips. And even then no word
of the ship, except as it might be this from
Hardenberg:

"What is it? Good God Almighty, I'm no
coward, but this thing is getting one too many
for me."

Then without further speech he went on
deck.

The air was cool. The sun was not yet up.
It was that strange, queer mid-period between
dark and dawn, when the night is over and the
day not yet come, just the gray that is neither
light nor dark, the dim dead blink as of the
refracted light from extinct worlds.

We stood at the rail. We did not speak;
we stood watching. It was so still that the
drip of steam from some loosened pipe far
below was plainly audible, and it sounded in
that lifeless, silent grayness like—God knows
what—a death tick.

"You see," said the mate, speaking just above a whisper, "there's no mistake about it. She is moving—this way."

"Oh, a current, of course," Strokher tried to say cheerfully, "sets her toward us."

Would the morning never come?

Ally Bazan—his parents were Catholic—began to mutter to himself.

Then Hardenberg spoke aloud.

"I particularly don't want—that—out—there—to cross our bows. I don't want it to come to that. We must get some sails on her."

"And I put it to you as man to man," said Strokher, "where might be your wind."

He was right. The *Glarus* floated in absolute calm. On all that slab of ocean nothing moved but the Dead Ship.

She came on slowly; her bows, the high, clumsy bows pointed toward us, the water turning from her forefoot. She came on; she was near at hand. We saw her plainly—saw the rotted planks, the crumbling rigging, the rust-corroded metal-work, the broken rail, the gaping deck, and I could imagine that the clean water broke away from her sides in refluent wavelets as though in recoil from a thing unclean. She made no sound. No single thing stirred aboard the hulk of her—but she moved.

We were helpless. The *Glarus* could stir no

boat in any direction; we were chained to the spot. Nobody had thought to put out our lights, and they still burned on through the dawn, strangely out of place in their red-and-green garishness, like maskers surprised by daylight.

And in the silence of that empty ocean, in that queer half-light between dawn and day, at six o'clock, silent as the settling of the dead to the bottomless bottom of the ocean, gray as fog, lonely, blind, soulless, voiceless, the Dead Ship crossed our bows.

I do not know how long after this the Ship disappeared, or what was the time of day when we at last pulled ourselves together. But we came to some sort of decision at last. This was to go on—under sail. We were too close to the island now to turn back for—for a broken shaft.

The afternoon was spent fitting on the sails to her, and when after nightfall the wind at length came up fresh and favourable, I believe we all felt heartened and a deal more hardy—until the last canvas went aloft, and Hardenberg took the wheel.

We had drifted a good deal since the morning, and the bows of the *Glarus* were pointed homeward, but as soon as the breeze blew strong enough to get steerageway Hardenberg put

the wheel over and, as the booms swung across
the deck, headed for the island again.

We had not gone on this course half an hour—
no, not twenty minutes—before the wind
shifted a whole quarter of the compass and
took the *Glarus* square in the teeth, so that
there was nothing for it but to tack. And
then the strangest thing befell.

I will make allowance for the fact that there
was no centre-board nor keel to speak of to the
Glarus. I will admit that the sails upon a nine-
hundred-ton freighter are not calculated to
speed her, nor steady her. I will even admit
the possibility of a current that set from the
island toward us. All this may be true, yet the
Glarus should have advanced. We should
have made a wake.

And instead of this, our stolid, steady, trusty
old boat was—what shall I say?

I will say that no man may thoroughly understand a ship—after all. I will say that new
ships are cranky and unsteady; that old and
seasoned ships have their little crochets, their
little fussinesses that their skippers must learn
and humour if they are to get anything out of
them; that even the best ships may sulk at
times, shirk their work, grow unstable, per-
verse, and refuse to answer helm and handling.
And I will say that some ships that for years

have sailed blue water as soberly and as docilely
as a street-car horse has plodded the treadmill
of the 'tween-tracks, have been known to balk,
as stubbornly and as conclusively as any old
Bay Billy that ever wore a bell. I know this
has happened, because I have seen it. I saw,
for instance, the *Glarus* do it.

Quite literally and truly we could do nothing
with her. We will say, if you like, that that
great jar and wrench when the shaft gave way
shook her and crippled her. It is true, however, that whatever the cause may have been,
we could not force her toward the island. Of
course, we all said "current"; but why didn't
the log-line trail?

For three days and three nights we tried it.
And the *Glarus* heaved and plunged and shook
herself just as you have seen a horse plunge
and rear when his rider tries to force him at the
steam-roller.

I tell you I could feel the fabric of her tremble
and shudder from bow to stern-post, as though
she were in a storm; I tell you she fell off from
the wind, and broad-on drifted back from her
course till the sensation of her shrinking was
as plain as her own staring lights and a thing
pitiful to see.

We roweled her, and we crowded sail upon
her, and we coaxed and bullied and humoured

her, till the Three Crows, their fortune only a
plain sail two days ahead, raved and swore
like insensate brutes, or shall we say like
mahouts trying to drive their stricken elephant
upon the tiger—and all to no purpose. "Damn
the damned current and the damned luck and
the damned shaft and all," Hardenberg would
exclaim, as from the wheel he would catch the
Glarus falling off. "Go on, you old hooker—
you tub of junk! My God, you'd think she
was scared!"

Perhaps the *Glarus* was scared, perhaps not;
that point is debatable. But it was beyond
doubt of debate that Hardenberg was scared.

A ship that will not obey is only one degree
less terrible than a mutinous crew. And we
were in a fair way to have both. The stokers,
whom we had impressed into duty as A. B.'s,
were of course superstitious; and they knew
how the *Glarus* was acting, and it was only a
question of time before they got out of hand.

That was the end. We held a final conference in the cabin and decided that there was
no help for it—we must turn back.

And back we accordingly turned, and at
once the wind followed us, and the "current"
helped us, and the water churned under the
forefoot of the *Glarus*, and the wake whitened
under her stern, and the log-line ran out from

the trail and strained back as the ship worked homeward.

We had never a mishap from the time we finally swung her about; and, considering the circumstances, the voyage back to San Francisco was propitious.

But an incident happened just after we had started back. We were perhaps some five miles on the homeward track. It was early evening and Strokher had the watch. At about seven o'clock he called me up on the bridge.

"See her?" he said.

And there, far behind us, in the shadow of the twilight, loomed the Other Ship again, desolate, lonely beyond words. We were leaving her rapidly astern. Strokher and I stood looking at her till she dwindled to a dot. Then Strokher said:

"She's on post again."

And when months afterward we limped into the Golden Gate and cast anchor off the "Front" our crew went ashore as soon as discharged, and in half a dozen hours the legend was in every sailors' boarding-house and in every seaman's dive, from Barbary Coast to Black Tom's.

It is still there, and that is why no pilot will take the *Glarus* out, no captain will navigate

her, no stoker feed her fires, no sailor walk her
decks. The *Glarus* is suspect. She will never
smell blue water again, nor taste the trades.
She has seen a Ghost.

THE GHOST IN THE CROSSTREES

THE GHOST IN THE CROSSTREES

I

CYRUS RYDER, the President of the South Pacific Exploitation Company, had at last got hold of a "proposition"—all Ryder's schemes were, in his vernacular, "propositions"—that was not only profitable beyond precedent or belief, but that also was, wonderful to say, more or less legitimate. He had got an "island." He had not discovered it. Ryder had not felt a deck under his shoes for twenty years other than the promenade deck of the ferry-boat *San Rafael*, that takes him home to Berkeley every evening after "business hours." He had not discovered it, but "Old Rosemary," captain of the barkentine *Scottish Chief*, of Blyth, had done that very thing, and, dying before he was able to perfect the title, had made over his interest in it to his best friend and old comrade, Cyrus Ryder.

"Old Rosemary," I am told, first landed on the island—it is called Paa—in the later '60's. He established its location and took its latitude and longitude, but as minutes and degrees

mean nothing to the lay reader, let it be said that
the Island of Paa lies just below the equator,
some 200 miles west of the Gilberts and 1,600
miles due east from Brisbane, in Australia.
It is six miles long, three wide, and because of
the prevailing winds and precipitous character
of the coast can only be approached from the
west during December and January.

"Old Rosemary" landed on the island,
raised the American flag, had the crew witness
the document by virtue of which he made
himself the possessor, and then, returning to
San Francisco, forwarded to the Secretary of
State, at Washington, application for title.
This was withheld till it could be shown that no
other nation had a prior claim. While "Old
Rosemary" was working out the proof, he died,
and the whole matter was left in abeyance till
Cyrus Ryder took it up. By then there was
a new Secretary in Washington and times were
changed, so that the Government of Ryder's
native land was not so averse toward acquiring
Eastern possessions. The Secretary of State
wrote to Ryder to say that the application
would be granted upon furnishing a bond for
$50,000; and you may believe that the bond
was forthcoming.

For in the first report upon Paa, "Old Rosemary" had used the magic word "guano."

He averred, and his crew attested over their
sworn statements, that Paa was covered to
an average depth of six feet with the stuff, so
that this last and biggest of "Cy" Ryder's
propositions was a vast slab of an extremely
marketable product six feet thick, three miles
wide and six miles long.

But no sooner had the title been granted
when there came a dislocation in the proceedings
that until then had been going forward so
smoothly. Ryder called the Three Black
Crows to him at this juncture, one certain
afternoon in the month of April. They were
his best agents. The plums that the "Company" had at its disposal generally went to the
trio, and if any man could "put through" a dangerous and desperate piece of work, Strokher,
Hardenberg and Ally Bazan were those men.

Of late they had been unlucky, and the affair
of the contraband arms, which had ended in
failure of cataclysmic proportions, yet rankled
in Ryder's memory, but he had no one else to
whom he could intrust the present proposition
and he still believed Hardenberg to be the best
boss on his list.

If Paa was to be fought for, Hardenberg,
backed by Strokher and Ally Bazan, was the
man of all men for the job, for it looked as
though Ryder would not get the Island of Paa

without a fight after all, and nitrate beds were worth fighting for.

"You see, boys, it's this way," Ryder explained to the three as they sat around the spavined table in the grimy back room of Ryder's "office." "It's this way. There's a scoovy after Paa, I'm told; he says he was there before 'Rosemary,' which is a lie, and that his Gov'ment has given him title. He's got a kind of dough-dish up Portland way and starts for Paa as soon as ever he kin fit out. He's got no title, in course, but if he gits there afore we do and takes possession it'll take fifty years o' lawing an' injunctioning to git him off. So hustle is the word for you from the word 'go.' We got a good start o' the scoovy. He can't put to sea within a week, while over yonder in Oakland Basin there's the *Idaho Lass*, as good a schooner, boys, as ever wore paint, all ready but to fit her new sails on her. Ye kin do it in less than no time. The stores will be goin' into her while ye're workin', and within the week I expect to see the *Idaho Lass* showing her heels to the Presidio. You see the point now, boys. If ye beat the scoovy—his name is Petersen, and his boat is called the *Elftruda*—we're to the wind'ard of a pretty pot o' money. If he gets away before you do—well, there's no telling; we prob'ly lose the island."

II

About ten days before the morning set for their departure I went over to the Oakland Basin to see how the Three Black Crows were getting on.

Hardenberg welcomed me as my boat bumped alongside, and extending a great tarry paw, hauled me over the rail. The schooner was a wilderness of confusion, with the sails covering, apparently, nine-tenths of the decks, the remaining tenth encumbered by spars, cordage, tangled rigging, chains, cables and the like, all helter-skeltered together in such a haze of entanglements that my heart misgave me as I looked on it. Surely order would not issue from this chaos in four days' time with only three men to speed the work.

But Hardenberg was reassuring, and little Ally Bazan, the colonial, told me they would "snatch her shipshape in the shorter end o' two days, if so be they must."

I stayed with the Three Crows all that day and shared their dinner with them on the quarterdeck when, wearied to death with the strain of wrestling with the slatting canvas and ponderous boom, they at last threw themselves upon the hamper of "cold snack" I had brought off with me and pledged the success of the venture in tin dippers full of Pilsener.

"And I'm thinking," said Ally Bazan, "as 'ow ye might as well turn in along o' us on board 'ere, instead o' hykin' back to town to-night. There's a fairish set o' currents up and daown 'ere about this time o' dye, and ye'd find it a stiff bit o' rowing."

"We'll sling a hammick for you on the quarterdeck, m'son," urged Hardenberg.

And so it happened that I passed my first night aboard the *Idaho Lass*.

We turned in early. The Three Crows were very tired, and only Ally Bazan and I were left awake at the time when we saw the 8:30 ferry-boat negotiating for her slip on the Oakland side. Then we also went to bed.

And now it becomes necessary, for a better understanding of what is to follow, to mention with some degree of particularization the places and manners in which my three friends elected to take their sleep, as well as the condition and berth of the schooner *Idaho Lass*.

Hardenberg slept upon the quarterdeck, rolled up in an army blanket and a tarpaulin. Strokher turned in below in the cabin upon the fixed lounge by the dining-table, while Ally Bazan stretched himself in one of the bunks in the fo'c's'le.

As for the location of the schooner, she lay out in the stream, some three or four cables' length off the yards and docks of a ship-building concern. No other ship or boat of any description was anchored nearer than at least 300 yards. She was a fine, roomy vessel, three-masted, about 150 feet in length over all. She lay head up stream, and from where I lay by Hardenberg on the quarterdeck I could see her tops sharply outlined against the sky above the Golden Gate before I went to sleep.

I suppose it was very early in the morning—nearer two than three—when I awoke. Some movement on the part of Hardenberg—as I afterward found out—had aroused me. But I lay inert for a long minute trying to find out why I was not in my own bed, in my own home, and to account for the rushing, rippling sound of the tide eddies sucking and chuckling around the *Lass's* rudder-post.

Then I became aware that Hardenberg was awake. I lay in my hammock, facing the stern of the schooner, and as Hardenberg had made up his bed between me and the wheel he was directly in my line of vision when I opened my eyes, and I could see him without any other movement than that of raising the eyelids. Just now, as I drifted more and more into wakefulness, I grew proportionately puzzled and perplexed to account for a singularly strange demeanour and conduct on the part of my friend.

He was sitting up in his place, his knees drawn up under the blanket, one arm thrown around both, the hand of the other arm resting on the neck and supporting the weight of his body. He was broad awake. I could see the green shine of our riding lantern in his wide-open eyes, and from time to time I could hear him muttering to himself, "What is it? What is it? What the devil is it, anyhow?" But it was not his attitude, nor the fact of his being so broad awake at the unseasonable hour, nor yet his unaccountable words, that puzzled me the most. It was the man's eyes and the direction in which they looked that startled me.

His gaze was directed not upon anything on the deck of the boat, nor upon the surface of the water near it, but upon something behind me and at a great height in the air. I was not long in getting myself broad awake.

III

I ROLLED out on the deck and crossed over to where Hardenberg sat huddled in his blankets. "What the devil——" I began.

He jumped suddenly at the sound of my voice, then raised an arm and pointed toward the top of the foremast.

"D'ye see it?" he muttered. "Say, huh? D'ye see it? I thought I saw it last night, but I wasn't sure. But there's no mistake now. D'ye see it, Mr. Dixon?"

I looked where he pointed. The schooner was riding easily to anchor, the surface of the bay was calm, but overhead the high white sea-fog was rolling in. Against it the foremast stood out like the hand of an illuminated town clock, and not a detail of its rigging that was not as distinct as if etched against the sky.

And yet I saw nothing.

"Where?" I demanded, and again and again "where?"

"In the crosstrees," whispered Hardenberg. "Ah, look there."

He was right. Something was stirring there, something that I had mistaken for the furled

221

tops'l. At first it was but a formless bundle, but as Hardenberg spoke it stretched itself, it grew upright, it assumed an erect attitude, it took the outlines of a human being. From head to heel a casing housed it in, a casing that might have been anything at that hour of the night and in that strange place—a shroud, if you like, a winding-sheet—anything; and it is without shame that I confess to a creep of the most disagreeable sensation I have ever known as I stood at Hardenberg's side on that still, foggy night and watched the stirring of that nameless, formless shape standing gaunt and tall and grisly and wrapped in its winding-sheet upon the crosstrees of the foremast of the *Idaho Lass.*

We watched and waited breathless for an instant. Then the creature on the foremast laid a hand upon the lashings of the tops'l and undid them. Then it turned, slid to the deck by I know not what strange process, and, still hooded, still shrouded, still lapped about by its mummy-wrappings, seized a rope's end. In an instant the jib was set and stood on hard and billowing against the night wind. The tops'l followed. Then the figure moved forward and passed behind the companionway of the fo'c's'le.

We looked for it to appear upon the

other side, but looked in vain. We saw it no more that night.

What Hardenberg and I told each other between the time of the disappearing and the hour of breakfast I am now ashamed to recall. But at last we agreed to say nothing to the others—for the time being. Just after breakfast, however, we two had a few words by the wheel on the quarterdeck. Ally Bazan and Strokher were forward.

"The proper thing to do," said I—it was a glorious, exhilarating morning, and the sunlight was flooding every angle and corner of the schooner—"the proper thing to do is to sleep on deck by the foremast to-night with our pistols handy and interview the—party if it walks again."

"Oh, yes," cried Hardenberg heartily. "Oh, yes; that's the proper thing. Of course it is. No manner o' doubt about that, Mr. Dixon. Watch for the party—yes, with pistols. Of course it's the proper thing. But I know one man that ain't going to do no such thing."

"Well," I remember to have said reflectively, "well—I guess I know another."

But for all our resolutions to say nothing to the others about the night's occurrences, we forgot that the tops'l and jib were both set and both drawing.

"An' w'at might be the bloomin' notion o' setting the bloomin' kite and jib?" demanded Ally Bazan not half an hour after breakfast. Shamelessly Hardenberg, at a loss for an answer, feigned an interest in the grummets of the life-boat cover and left me to lie as best I might.

But it is not easy to explain why one should raise the sails of an anchored ship during the night, and Ally Bazan grew very suspicious. Strokher, too, had something to say, and in the end the whole matter came out.

Trust a sailor to give full value to anything savouring of the supernatural. Strokher promptly voted the ship a "queer old hooker anyhow, and about as seaworthy as a hen-coop." He held forth at great length upon the subject.

"You mark my words, now," he said. "There's been some fishy doin's in this 'ere vessel, and it's like somebody done to death crool hard, an' 'e wants to git away from the smell o' land, just like them as is killed on blue water. That's w'y 'e takes an' sets the sails between dark an' dawn."

But Ally Bazan was thoroughly and wholly upset, so much so that at first he could not speak. He went pale and paler while we stood talking it over, and crossed himself—he

was a Catholic—furtively behind the water-
butt.

"I ain't never 'a' been keen on ha'nts anyhow,
Mr. Dixon," he told me aggrievedly at dinner
that evening. "I got no use for 'em. I ain't
never known any good to come o' anything
with a ha'nt tagged to it, an' we're makin' a
ill beginnin' o' this island business, Mr. Dixon
—a blyme ill beginnin'. I mean to stye awyke
to-night."

But if he was awake the little colonial was
keeping close to his bunk at the time when
Strokher and Hardenberg woke me at about
three in the morning.

I rolled out and joined them on the quarterdeck and stood beside them watching. The
same figure again towered, as before, gray and
ominous in the crosstrees. As before, it set
the tops'l; as before, it came down to the deck
and raised the jib; as before, it passed out of
sight amid the confusion of the forward deck.

But this time we all ran toward where we
last had seen it, stumbling over the encumbered
decks, jostling and tripping, but keeping
wonderfully close together. It was not twenty
seconds from the time the creature had disappeared before we stood panting upon the
exact spot we had last seen it. We searched
every corner of the forward deck in vain. We

looked over the side. The moon was up.
This night there was no fog. We could see
for miles each side of us, but never a trace of a
boat was visible, and it was impossible that any
swimmer could have escaped the merciless
scrutiny to which we subjected the waters of
the bay in every direction.

Hardenberg and I dived down into the
fo'c's'le. Ally Bazan was sound asleep in his
bunk and woke stammering, blinking and
bewildered by the lantern we carried.

"I sye," he cried, all at once scrambling up
and clawing at our arms, "D'd the bally ha'nt
show up agyne?" And as we nodded he went
on more aggrievedly than ever—"Oh, I sye, y'
know, I daon't like this. I eyen't shipping in
no bloomin' 'ooker wot carries a ha'nt for
supercargo. They waon't no good come o'
this cruise—no, they waon't. It's a sign, that's
wot it is. I eyen't goin' to buck again no signs
—it eyen't human nature, no it eyen't. You
mark my words, 'Bud' Hardenberg, we clear
this port with a ship wot has a ha'nt an' we
waon't never come back agyne, my hearty."

That night he berthed aft with us on the
quarterdeck, but though we stood watch and
watch till well into the dawn, nothing stirred
about the foremast. So it was the next night,
and so the night after that. When three

successive days had passed without any manifes-
tation the keen edge of the business became
a little blunted and we declared that an end
had been made.

Ally Bazan returned to his bunk in the
fo'c's'le on the fourth night, and the rest of
us slept the hours through unconcernedly.

But in the morning there were the jib and
tops'l set and drawing as before.

IV

AFTER this we began experimenting—on Ally
Bazan. We bunked him forward and we
bunked him aft, for some one had pointed out
that the "ha'nt walked only at the times when
the colonial slept in the fo'c's'le. We found this
to be true. Let the little fellow watch on the
quarterdeck with us and the night passed without disturbance. As soon as he took up his
quarters forward the haunting recommenced.
Furthermore, it began to appear that the
"ha'nt" carefully refrained from appearing to
him. He of us all had never seen the thing.
He of us all was spared the chills and the
harrowings that laid hold upon the rest of us
during these still gray hours after midnight
when we huddled on the deck of the *Idaho Lass*
and watched the sheeted apparition in the
rigging; for by now there was no more charging
forward in attempts to run the ghost down.
We had passed that stage long since.

But so far from rejoicing in this immunity or
drawing courage therefrom, Ally Bazan filled
the air with his fears and expostulations. Just
the fact that he was in some way differentiated

229

from the others—that he was singled out, if
only for exemption—worked upon him. And
that he was unable to scale his terrors by actual
sight of their object excited them all the more.

And there issued from this a curious conse-
quence. He, the very one who had never seen
the haunting, was also the very one to unsettle
what little common sense yet remained to
Hardenberg and Strokher. He never allowed
the subject to be ignored—never lost an oppor-
tunity of referring to the doom that o'erhung
the vessel. By the hour he poured into the
ears of his friends lugubrious tales of ships,
warned as this one was, that had cleared from
port, never to be seen again. He recalled to
their minds parallel incidents that they themselves had heard; he foretold the fate of the
Idaho Lass when the land should lie behind and
she should be alone in midocean with this
horrid supercargo that took liberties with the
rigging, and at last one particular morning, two
days before that which was to witness the
schooner's departure, he came out flatfooted
to the effect that "Gaw-blyme him, he couldn't
stand the gaff no longer, no he couldn't, so help
him, that if the owners were wishful for to put
to sea" (doomed to some unnamable destruc-
tion) "he for one wa'n't fit to die, an' was
going to quit that blessed day."

For the sake of appearances, Hardenberg and Strokher blustered and fumed, but I could hear the crack in Strokher's voice as plain as in a broken ship's bell. I was not surprised at what happened later in the day, when he told the others that he was a very sick man. A congenital stomach trouble, it seemed— or was it liver complaint—had found him out again. He had contracted it when a lad at Trincomalee, diving for pearls; it was acutely painful, it appeared. Why, gentlemen, even at that very moment, as he stood there talking —Hi, yi! O Lord!—talking, it was a-griping of him something uncommon, so it was. And no, it was no manner of use for him to think of going on this voyage; sorry he was, too, for he'd made up his mind, so he had, to find out just what was wrong with the foremast, etc.

And thereupon Hardenberg swore a great oath and threw down the capstan bar he held in his hand.

"Well, then," he cried wrathfully, "we might as well chuck up the whole business. No use going to sea with a sick man and a scared man."

"An' there's the first word o' sense," cried Ally Bazan, "I've heard this long day. 'Scared,' he says; aye, right ye are, me bully."

"It's Cy Rider's fault," the three declared

after a two-hours' talk. "No business giving
us a schooner with a ghost aboard. Scoovy
or no scoovy, island or no island, guano or
no guano, we don't go to sea in the haunted
hooker called the *Idaho Lass*."

No more they did. On board the schooner
they had faced the supernatural with some
kind of courage born of the occasion. Once
on shore, and no money could hire, no power
force them to go aboard a second time.

The affair ended in a grand wrangle in
Cy Rider's back office, and just twenty-four
hours later the bark *Elftruda*, Captain Jens
Petersen, cleared from Portland, bound for
"a cruise to South Pacific ports—in ballast."

.   .   .   .   .   .

Two years after this I took Ally Bazan with
me on a duck-shooting excursion in the "Toolies"
back of Sacramento, for he is a handy man
about a camp and can row a boat as softly
as a drifting cloud.

We went about in a cabin cat of some thirty
feet over all, the rowboat towing astern. Sometimes we did not go ashore to camp, but slept
aboard. On the second night of this expedient
I woke in my blankets on the floor of the
cabin to see the square of gray light that stood
for the cabin door darkened by—it gave me
the same old start—a sheeted figure. It was

going up the two steps to the deck. Beyond question it had been in the cabin. I started up and followed it. I was too frightened not to—if you can see what I mean. By the time I had got the blankets off and had thrust my head above the level of the cabin hatch the figure was already in the bows, and, as a matter of course, hoisting the jib.

I thought of calling Ally Bazan, who slept by me on the cabin floor, but it seemed to me at the time that if I did not keep that figure in sight it would elude me again, and, besides, if I went back in the cabin I was afraid that I would bolt the door and remain under the bedclothes till morning. I was afraid to go on with the adventure, but I was much more afraid to go back.

So I crept forward over the deck of the sloop. The "ha'nt" had its back toward me, fumbling with the ends of the jib halyards. I could hear the creak of new ropes as it undid the knot, and the sound was certainly substantial and commonplace. I was so close by now that I could see every outline of the shape. It was precisely as it had appeared on the crosstrees of the *Idaho*, only, seen without perspective, and brought down to the level of the eye, it lost its exaggerated height.

It had been kneeling upon the deck. Now,

at last, it rose and turned about, the end of the halyards in its hand. The light of the earliest dawn fell squarely on the face and form, and I saw, if you please, Ally Bazan himself. His eyes were half shut, and through his open lips came the sound of his deep and regular breathing.

At breakfast the next morning I asked, "Ally Bazan, did you ever walk in your sleep."

"Aye," he answered, "years ago, when I was by wye o' being a lad, I used allus to wrap the bloomin' sheets around me. An' crysy things I'd do the times. But the 'abit left me when I grew old enough to tyke me whisky strite and have hair on me fyce."

I did not "explain away" the ghost in the crosstrees either to Ally Bazan or to the other two Black Crows. Furthermore, I do not now refer to the Island of Paa in the hearing of the trio. The claims and title of Norway to the island have long since been made good and conceded—even by the State Department at Washington—and I understand that Captain Petersen has made a very pretty fortune out of the affair.

THE RIDING OF FELIPE

THE RIDING OF FELIPE

I

FELIPE

AS young Felipe Arillaga guided his pony out of the last intricacies of Pacheco Pass, he was thinking of Rubia Ytuerate and of the scene he had had with her a few days before. He reconstructed it now very vividly. Rubia had been royally angry, and as she had stood before him, her arms folded and her teeth set, he was forced to admit that she was as handsome a woman as could be found through all California.

There had been a time, three months past, when Felipe found no compulsion in the admission, for though betrothed to Buelna Martiarena he had abruptly conceived a violent infatuation for Rubia, and had remained a guest upon her rancho many weeks longer than he had intended.

For three months he had forgotten Buelna entirely. At the end of that time he had remembered her—had awakened to the fact that his infatuation for Rubia was infatuation,

237

and had resolved to end the affair and go back
to Buelna as soon as it was possible.

But Rubia was quick to notice the cooling
of his passion. First she fixed him with oblique
suspicion from under her long lashes, then
avoided him, then kept him at her side for days
together. Then at last—his defection unmistakable—turned on him with furious demands
for the truth.

Felipe had snatched occasion with one hand
and courage with the other.

"Well," he had said, "well, it is not my
fault. Yes, it is the truth. It is played out."

He had not thought it necessary to speak
of Buelna; but Rubia divined the other
woman.

"So you think you are to throw me aside
like that. Ah, it is played out, is it, Felipe
Arillaga? You listen to me. Do not fancy
for one moment you are going back to an old
love, or on to a new one. You listen to me,"
she had cried, her fist over her head. "I do
not know who she is, but my curse is on her,
Felipe Arillaga. My curse is on her who next
kisses you. May that kiss be a blight to her.
From that moment may evil cling to her,
bad luck follow her; may she love and not be
loved; may friends desert her, enemies beset
her, her sisters shame her, her brothers dis-

"'MY CURSE IS ON HER WHO NEXT KISSES YOU'"

own her, and those whom she has loved abandon her. May her body waste as your love for me has wasted; may her heart be broken as your promises to me have been broken; may her joy be as fleeting as your vows, and her beauty grow as dim as your memory of me. I have said it."

"So be it !" Felipe had retorted with vast nonchalance, and had flung out from her presence to saddle his pony and start back to Buelna.

But Felipe was superstitious. He half believed in curses, had seen two-headed calves born because of them, and sheep stampeded over cliffs for no other reason.

Now, as he drew out of Pacheco Pass and came down into the valley the idea of Rubia and her curse troubled him. At first, when yet three days' journey from Buelna, it had been easy to resolve to brave it out. But now he was already on the Rancho Martiarena (had been traveling over it for the last ten hours, in fact), and in a short time would be at the *hacienda* of Martiarena, uncle and guardian of Buelna. He would see Buelna, and she, believing always in his fidelity, would expect to kiss him.

"Well, this is to be thought about," murmured Felipe uneasily.

He touched up the pony with one of his enormous spurs.

"Now I know what I will do," he thought. "I will go to San Juan Bautista and confess and be absolved, and will buy candles. Then afterward will go to Buelna."

He found the road that led to the Mission and turned into it, pushing forward at a canter. Then suddenly at a sharp turning reined up just in time to avoid colliding with a little cavalcade.

He uttered an exclamation under his breath.

At the head of the cavalcade rode old Martiarena himself, and behind him came a *peon* or two, then Manuela, the aged housekeeper and —after a fashion—duenna. Then at her side, on a saddle of red leather with silver bosses, which was cinched about the body of a very small white burro, Buelna herself.

She was just turned sixteen, and being of the best blood of the mother kingdom (the strain dating back to the Ostrogothic invasion), was fair. Her hair was blond, her eyes blue-gray, her eyebrows and lashes dark brown, and as he caught sight of her Felipe wondered how he ever could have believed the swarthy Rubia beautiful.

There was a jubilant meeting. Old Martiarena kissed both his cheeks, patting him on the back.

"Oh, ho!" he cried. "Once more back. We have just returned from the feast of the Santa Cruz at the Mission, and Buelna prayed for your safe return. Go to her, boy. She has waited long for this hour."

Felipe, his eyes upon those of his betrothed, advanced. She was looking at him and smiling. As he saw the unmistakable light in her blue eyes, the light he knew she had kept burning for him alone, Felipe could have abased himself to the very hoofs of her burro. Could it be possible he had ever forgotten her for such a one as Rubia—have been unfaithful to this dear girl for so much as the smallest fraction of a minute?

"You are welcome, Felipe," she said. "Oh, very, very welcome." She gave him her hand and turned her face to his. But it was her hand and not her face the young man kissed. Old Martiarena, who looked on, shook with laughter.

"Hoh! a timid lover this," he called. "We managed different when I was a lad. Her lips, Felipe. Must an old man teach a youngster gallantry?"

Buelna blushed and laughed, but yet did not withdraw her hand nor turn her face away.

There was a delicate expectancy in her manner that she nevertheless contrived to make compatible with her native modesty. Felipe had been her acknowledged lover ever since, the two were children.

"Well?" cried Martiarena as Felipe hesitated.

Even then, if Felipe could have collected his wits, he might have saved the situation for himself. But no time had been allowed him to think. Confusion seized upon him. All that was clear in his mind were the last words of Rubia. It seemed to him that between his lips he carried a poison deadly to Buelna above all others. Stupidly, brutally he precipitated the catastrophe.

"No," he exclaimed seriously, abruptly drawing his hand from Buelna's, "no. It may not be. I cannot."

Martiarena stared. Then:

"Is this a jest, señor?" he demanded. "An ill-timed one, then."

"No," answered Felipe, "it is not a jest."

"But, Felipe," murmured Buelna. "But—why—I do not understand."

"I think I begin to," cried Martiarena.

"Señor, you do not," protested Felipe. "It is not to be explained. I know what you believe. On my honour, I love Buelna."

"Your actions give you the lie, then, young

man. Bah! Nonsense. What fool's play is
all this? Kiss him, Buelna, and have done
with it."

Felipe gnawed his nails.

"Believe me, oh, believe me, Señor Martiarena, it must not be."

"Then an explanation."

For a moment Felipe hesitated. But how
could he tell them the truth—the truth that
involved Rubia and his disloyalty, temporary
though that was. They could neither understand nor forgive. Here, indeed, was an
impasse. One thing only was to be said, and
he said it. "I can give you no explanation,"
he murmured.

But Buelna suddenly interposed.

"Oh, please," she said, pushing by Felipe,
"uncle, we have talked too long. Please let
us go. There is only one explanation. Is it
not enough already?"

"By God, it is not!" vociferated the old
man, turning upon Felipe. "Tell me what it
means. Tell me what this means."

"I cannot."

"Then I will tell *you!*" shouted the old fellow
in Felipe's face. "It means that you are a liar
and a rascal. That you have played with
Buelna, and that you have deceived me, who
have trusted you as a father would have

trusted a son. I forbid you to answer me.
For the sake of what you were I spare you
now. But this I will do. Off of my
rancho!" he cried. "Off my rancho, and
in the future pray your God, or the devil, to
whom you are sold, to keep you far from me."

"You do not understand, you do not understand," pleaded Felipe, the tears starting to
his eyes. "Oh, believe me, I speak the truth.
I love your niece. I love Buelna. Oh, never
so truly, never so devoutly as now. Let me
speak to her; she will believe me."

But Buelna, weeping, had ridden on.

II

A FORTNIGHT passed. Soon a month had gone by. Felipe gloomed about his rancho, solitary, taciturn, siding the sheep-walks and cattle-ranges for days and nights together, refusing all intercourse with his friends. It seemed as if he had lost Buelna for good and all. At times, as the certainty of this defined itself more clearly, Felipe would fling his hat upon the ground, beat his breast, and then, prone upon his face, his head buried in his folded arms, would lie for hours motionless, while his pony nibbled the sparse alfalfa, and the jack-rabbits limping from the sage peered at him, their noses wrinkling.

But about a month after the meeting and parting with Buelna, word went through all the ranches that a hide-roger had cast anchor in Monterey Bay. At once an abrupt access of activity seized upon the rancheros. Rodéos were held, sheep slaughtered, and the great tallow-pits began to fill up.

Felipe was not behind his neighbours, and,

245

his tallow once in hand, sent it down to Monterey, and himself rode down to see about disposing of it.

On his return he stopped at the wine shop of one Lopez Catala, on the road between Monterey and his rancho.

It was late afternoon when he reached it, and the wine shop was deserted. Outside, the California August lay withering and suffocating over all the land. The far hills were burnt to dry, hay-like grass and brittle clods. The eucalyptus trees in front of the wine shop (the first trees Felipe had seen all that day) were coated with dust. The plains of sage-brush and the alkali flats shimmered and exhaled pallid mirages, glistening like inland seas. Over all blew the trade-wind; prolonged, insistent, harassing, swooping up the red dust of the road and the white powder of the alkali beds, and flinging it—white-and-red banners in a sky of burnt-out blue—here and there about the landscape.

The wine shop, which was also an inn, was isolated, lonely, but it was comfortable, and Felipe decided to lay over there that night, then in the morning reach his rancho by an easy stage.

He had his supper—an omelet, cheese, tortillas, and a glass of wine—and afterward sat outside on a bench smoking innumerable cigarettes and watching the sun set.

While he sat so a young man of about his own age rode up from the eastward with a great flourish, and giving over his horse to the *muchacho*, entered the wine shop and ordered dinner and a room for the night. Afterward he came out and stood in front of the inn and watched the *muchacho* cleaning his horse.

Felipe, looking at him, saw that he was of his own age and about his own build—that is to say, twenty-eight or thirty, and tall and lean. But in other respects the difference was great. The stranger was flamboyantly dressed: skin-tight pantaloons, fastened all up and down the leg with round silver buttons; yellow boots with heels high as a girl's, set off with silver spurs; a very short coat faced with galloons of gold, and a very broad-brimmed and very high-crowned sombrero, on which the silver braid alone was worth the price of a good horse. Even for a Spanish Mexican his face was dark. Swart it was, the cheeks hollow; a tiny, tight mustache with ends truculently pointed and erect helped out the belligerency of the tight-shut lips. The eyes were black as bitumen, and flashed continually under heavy brows.

"Perhaps," thought Felipe, "he is a *toreador* from Mexico."

The stranger followed his horse to the barn, but, returning in a few moments, stood before Felipe and said:

"Señor, I have taken the liberty to put my horse in the stall occupied by yours. Your beast the *muchacho* turned into the *corrale*. Mine is an animal of spirit, and in a *corrale* would fight with the other horses. I rely upon the señor's indulgence."

At ordinary times he would not have relied in vain. But Felipe's nerves were in a jangle these days, and his temper, since Buelna's dismissal of him, was bitter. His perception of offense was keen. He rose, his eyes upon the stranger's eyes.

"My horse is mine," he observed. "Only my friends permit themselves liberties with what is mine."

The other smiled scornfully and drew from his belt a little pouch of gold dust.

"What I take I pay for," he remarked, and, still smiling, tendered Felipe a few grains of the gold.

Felipe struck the outstretched palm.

"Am I a *peon?*" he vociferated.

"Probably," retorted the other.

"I *will* take pay for that word," cried Felipe,

his face blazing, "but not in your money, señor."

"In that case I may give you more than you ask."

"No, by God, for I shall take all you have." But the other checked his retort. A sudden change came over him.

"I ask the señor's pardon," he said, with grave earnestness, "for provoking him. You may not fight with me nor I with you. I speak the truth. I have made oath not to fight till I have killed one whom now I seek."

"Very well; I, too, spoke without reflection. You seek an enemy, then, señor?"

"My sister's, who is therefore mine. An enemy truly. Listen, you shall judge. I am absent from my home a year, and when I return what do I find? My sister betrayed, deceived, flouted by a fellow, a nobody, whom she received a guest in her house, a fit return for kindness, for hospitality! Well, he answers to me for the dishonour."

"Wait. Stop!" interposed Felipe. "Your name, señor."

"Unzar Ytuerate, and my enemy is called Arillaga. Him I seek and——"

"Then you shall seek no farther!" shouted Felipe. "It is to Rubia Ytuerate, your sister, whom I owe all my unhappiness, all my suffering.

She has hurt not me only, but one—but——
Mother of God, we waste words!" he cried.
"Knife to knife, Unzar Ytuerate. I am Felipe
Arillaga, and may God be thanked for the
chance that brings this quarrel to my hand."

"You! You!" gasped Unzar. Fury choked
him; his hands clutched and unclutched—
now fists, now claws. His teeth grated sharply
while a quivering sensation as of a chill crisped
his flesh. "Then the sooner the better," he
muttered between his set teeth, and the knives
flashed in the hands of the two men so suddenly
that the gleam of one seemed only the reflection of the other.

Unzar held out his left wrist.

"Are you willing?" he demanded, with
a significant glance.

"And ready," returned the other, baring his
forearm.

Catala, keeper of the inn, was called.

"Love of the Virgin, not here, señors. My
house—the *alcalde*——"

"You have a strap there." Unzar pointed
to a bridle hanging from a peg by the
doorway. "No words; quick; do as you
are told."

The two men held out their left arms till
wrist touched wrist, and Catala, trembling and
protesting, lashed them together with a strap.

"Tighter," commanded Felipe; "put all your strength to it."

The strap was drawn up to another hole.

"Now, Catala, stand back," commanded Unzar, "and count three slowly. At the word 'three,' Señor Arillaga, we begin. You understand."

"I understand."

"Ready. . . . Count."

"One."

Felipe and Unzar each put his right hand grasping the knife behind his back as etiquette demanded.

"Two."

They strained back from each other, the full length of their left arms, till the nails grew bloodless.

"*Three!*" called Lopez Catala in a shaking voice.

III

RUBIA

WHEN Felipe regained consciousness he found that he lay in an upper chamber of Catala's inn upon a bed. His shoulder, the right one, was bandaged, and so was his head. He felt no pain, only a little weak, but there was a comfortable sense of brandy at his lips, an arm supported his head, and the voice of Rubia Ytuerate spoke his name. He sat up on a sudden.

"Rubia, *you !*" he cried. "What is it? What happened? Oh, I remember, Unzar— we fought. Oh, my God, how we fought! But you—— What brought you here?"

"Thank Heaven," she murmured, "you are better. You are not so badly wounded. As he fell he must have dragged you with him, and your head struck the threshold of the doorway."

"Is he badly hurt? Will he recover?"

"I hope so. But *you* are safe."

"But what brought you here?"

"Love," she cried; "my love for you. What

I suffered after you had gone! Felipe, I have
fought, too. Pride was strong at first, and it
was pride that made me send Unzar after you.
I told him what had happened. I hounded
him to hunt you down. Then when he had
gone my battle began. Ah, dearest, dearest,
it all came back, our days together, the life
we led, knowing no other word but love, thinking no thoughts that were not of each other.
And love conquered. Unzar was not a week
gone before I followed him—to call him back,
to shield you, to save you from his fury. I
came all but too late, and found you both half
dead. My brother and my lover, your body
across his, your blood mingling with his own.
But not too late to love you back to life again.
Your life is mine now, Felipe. I love you,
I love you." She clasped her hands together
and pressed them to her cheek. "Ah, if you
knew," she cried; "if you could only look into
my heart. Pride is nothing; good name is
nothing; friends are nothing. Oh, it is a
glory to give them all for love, to give up
everything; to surrender, to submit, to cry to
one's heart: 'Take me; I am as wax. Take me;
conquer me; lead me wherever you will. All
is well lost so only that love remains.' And
I have heard all that has happened—this other
one, the Señorita Buelna, how that she for-

bade you her lands. Let her go; she is not
worthy of your love, cold, selfish———"

"Stop!" cried Felipe, "you shall say no
more evil of her. It is enough."

"Felipe, you love her yet?"

"And always, always will."

"She who has cast you off; she who disdains
you, who will not suffer you on her lands?
And have *you* come to be so low, so base and
mean as that?"

"I have sunk no lower than a woman who
could follow after a lover who had grown
manifestly cold."

"Ah," she answered sadly, "if I could so
forget my pride as to follow you, do not think
your reproaches can touch me now." Then
suddenly she sank at the bedside and clasped
his hand in both of hers. Her beautiful hair,
unbound, tumbled about her shoulders; her
eyes, swimming with tears, were turned up to
his; her lips trembled with the intensity of her
passion. In a voice low, husky, sweet as a
dove's, she addressed him. "Oh, dearest, come
back to me; come back to me. Let me love
you again. Don't you see my heart is break-
ing? There is only you in all the world for
me. I was a proud woman once. See now
what I have brought myself to. Don't let it
all be in vain. If you fail me now, think how

it will be for me afterward—to know that I—
I, Rubia Ytuerate, have begged the love of a
man and begged in vain. Do you think I
could live knowing that?" Abruptly she lost
control of herself. She caught him about the
neck with both her arms. Almost incoherently
her words rushed from her tight-shut teeth.

"Ah, I can *make* you love me. I can make
you love me," she cried. "You shall come back
to me. You are mine, and you cannot help
but come back."

"*Por Dios*, Rubia," he ejaculated, "remember yourself. You are out of your head."

"Come back to me; love me."

"No, no."

"Come back to me."

"No."

"You cannot push me from you," she cried,
for, one hand upon her shoulder, he had sought
to disengage himself. "No, I shall not let
you go. You shall not push me from you!
Thrust me off and I will embrace you all the
closer. Yes, *strike* me if you will, and I will
kiss you."

And with the words she suddenly pressed
her lips to his.

Abruptly Felipe freed himself. A new
thought suddenly leaped to his brain.

"Let your own curse return upon you,"

he cried. "You yourself have freed me; you
yourself have broken the barrier you raised
between me and my betrothed. You cursed
her whose lips should next touch mine, and
you are poisoned with your own venom."

He sprang from off the bed, and catching up
his *serape*, flung it about his shoulders.

"Felipe," she cried, "Felipe, where are you
going?"

"Back to Buelna," he shouted, and with the
words rushed from the room. Her strength
seemed suddenly to leave her. She sank lower
to the floor, burying her face deep upon the
pillows that yet retained the impress of him
she loved so deeply, so recklessly.

Footsteps in the passage and a knocking at
the door aroused her. A woman, one of the
escort who had accompanied her, entered
hurriedly.

"Señorita," cried this one, "your brother,
the Señor Unzar, he is dying."

Rubia hurried to an adjoining room, where
upon a mattress on the floor lay her brother.

"Put that woman out," he gasped as his
glance met hers. "I never sent for her," he
went on. "You are no longer sister of mine.
It was you who drove me to this quarrel, and
when I have vindicated you what do you do?
Your brother you leave to be tended by hire-

lings, while all your thought and care are lavished on your paramour. Go back to him. I know how to die alone, but as you go remember that in dying I hated and disowned you."

He fell back upon the pillows, livid, dead.

Rubia started forward with a cry.

"It is you who have killed him," cried the woman who had summoned her. The rest of Rubia's escort, *vaqueros*, *peons*, and the old *alcalde* of her native village, stood about with bared heads.

"That is true. That is true," they murmured. The old *alcalde* stepped forward.

"Who dishonours my friend dishonours me," he said. "From this day, Señorita Ytuerate, you and I are strangers." He went out, and one by one, with sullen looks and hostile demeanour, Rubia's escort followed. Their manner was unmistakable; they were deserting her.

Rubia clasped her hands over her eyes.

"*Madre de Dios, Madre de Dios*," she moaned over and over again. Then in a low voice she repeated her own words: "May it be a blight to her. From that moment may evil cling to her, bad luck follow her; may she love and not be loved; may friends desert her, her sisters shame her, her brothers disown her——"

There was a clatter of horse's hoofs in the courtyard.

"It is your lover," said her woman coldly from the doorway. "He is riding away from you."

"——and those," added Rubia, "whom she has loved abandon her."

IV

M<small>EANWHILE</small> Felipe, hatless, bloody, was galloping through the night, his pony's head
turned toward the *hacienda* of Martiarena.
The Rancho Martiarena lay between his own
rancho and the inn where he had met Rubia,
so that this distance was not great. He
reached it in about an hour of vigorous
spurring.

The place was dark though it was as yet
early in the night, and an ominous gloom
seemed to hang about the house. Felipe, his
heart sinking, pounded at the door, and at
last aroused the aged superintendent, who was
also a sort of *major-domo* in the household, and
who in Felipe's boyhood had often ridden him
on his knee.

"Ah, it is you, Arillaga," he said very sadly,
as the moonlight struck across Felipe's face.
"I had hoped never to see you again."

"Buelna," demanded Felipe. "I have something to say to her, and to the *padron*."

"Too late, señor."

261

"My God, dead?"

"As good as dead."

"Rafael, tell me all. I have come to set everything straight again. On my honour, I have been misjudged. Is Buelna well?"

"Listen. You know your own heart best, señor. When you left her our little lady was as one half dead; her heart died within her. Ah, she loved you, Arillaga, far more than you deserved. She drooped swiftly, and one night all but passed away. Then it was that she made a vow that if God spared her life she would become the bride of the church—would forever renounce the world. Well, she recovered, became almost well again, but not the same as before. She never will be that. So soon as she was able to obtain Martiarena's consent she made all the preparations—signed away all her lands and possessions, and spent the days and nights in prayer and purifications. The Mother Superior of the Convent of Santa Teresa has been a guest at the *hacienda* this fortnight past. Only to-day the party—that is to say, Martiarena, the Mother Superior and Buelna—left for Santa Teresa, and at midnight of this very night Buelna takes the veil. You know your own heart, Señor Felipe. Go your way."

"But not *till* midnight!" cried Felipe.

"What? I do not understand."

"She will not take the veil till midnight."

"No, not till then."

"Rafael," cried Felipe, "ask me no questions now. Only *believe* me. I always have and always will love Buelna. I swear it. I can stop this yet; only once let me reach her in time. Trust me. Ah, for this once trust me, you who have known me since I was a lad."

He held out his hand. The other for a moment hesitated, then impulsively clasped it in his own.

"*Bueno*, I trust you then. Yet I warn you not to fool me twice."

"Good," returned Felipe. "And now *adios*. Unless I bring her back with me you'll never see me again."

"But, Felipe, lad, where away now?"

"To Santa Teresa."

"You are mad. Do you fancy you can reach it before midnight?" insisted the *major-domo*.

"I *will*, Rafael; I *will*."

"Then Heaven be with you."

But the old fellow's words were lost in a wild clatter of hoofs, as Felipe swung his pony around and drove home the spurs. Through the night came back a cry already faint:

"*Adios, adios.*"

"*Adios*, Felipe," murmured the old man as he stood bewildered in the doorway, "and your good angel speed you now."

When Felipe began his ride it was already a little after nine. Could he reach Santa Teresa before midnight? The question loomed grim before him, but he answered only with the spur. Pépe was hardy, and, as Felipe well knew, of indomitable pluck. But what a task now lay before the little animal. He might do it, but oh! it was a chance!

In a quarter of a mile Pépe had settled to his stride, the dogged, even gallop that Felipe knew so well, and at half-past ten swung through the main street of Piedras Blancas—silent, somnolent, dark.

"Steady, little Pépe," said Felipe; "steady, little one. Soh, soh. There."

The little horse flung back an ear, and Felipe could feel along the lines how he felt for the bit, trying to get a grip of it to ease the strain on his mouth.

The *De Profundis* bell was sounding from the church tower as Felipe galloped through San Anselmo, the next village, but by the time he raised the lights of Arcata it was black night in very earnest. He set his teeth. Terra Bella lay eight miles farther ahead, and here from the town-hall clock that looked down upon the plaza he would be able to know the time.

"*Hoopa, Pépe; pronto!*" he shouted.

The pony responded gallantly. His head was low; his ears in constant movement, twitched restlessly back and forth, now laid flat on his neck, now cocked to catch the rustle of the wind in the chaparral, the scurrying of a rabbit or ground-owl through the sage.

It grew darker, colder, the trade-wind lapsed away. Low in the sky upon the right a pale, dim belt foretold the rising of the moon. The incessant galloping of the pony was the only sound.

The convent toward which he rode was just outside the few scattered huts in the valley of the Rio Esparto that by charity had been invested with the name of Caliente. From Piedras Blancas to Caliente between twilight and midnight! What a riding! Could he do it? Would Pépe last under him?

"Steady, little one. Steady, Pépe."

Thus he spoke again and again, measuring the miles in his mind, husbanding the little fellow's strength.

Lights! Cart lanterns? No, Terra Bella. A great dog charged out at him from a dobe, filling the night with outcry; a hayrick loomed by like a ship careening through fog; there was a smell of chickens and farmyards. Then a paved street, an open square, a solitary pedestrian dodging just in time from under Pépe's hools. All flashed by. The open country again, unbroken darkness again, and solitude of the fields again. Terra Bella past.

But through the confusion Felipe retained one picture, that of the moon-faced clock with hands marking the hour of ten. On again with Pépe leaping from the touch of the spur. On again up the long, shallow slope that rose for miles to form the divide that overlooked the valley of the Esparto.

"Hold, there! Madman to ride thus. Mad or drunk. Only desperadoes gallop at night. Halt and speak!"

The pony had swerved barely in time, and behind him the Monterey stage lay all but ditched on the roadside, the driver fulminating oaths. But Felipe gave him but an instant's thought. Dobe huts once more abruptly ranged up on either side the roadway, staggering and dim under the night. Then a wine shop noisy with carousing *peons* darted by. Pavements again. A shop-front or two. A pig snoring in the gutter, a dog howling in a yard, a cat lamenting on a rooftop. Then the smell of fields again. Then darkness again. Then the solitude of the open country. Cadenassa past.

But now the country changed. The slope
grew steeper; it was the last lift of land to the
divide. The road was sown with stones and
scored with ruts. Pépe began to blow; once
he groaned. Perforce his speed diminished.
The villages were no longer so thickly spread
now. The crest of the divide was wild, desolate, forsaken. Felipe again and again searched
the darkness for lights, but the night was black.

Then abruptly the moon rose. By that
Felipe could guess the time. His heart sank.
He halted, recinched the saddle, washed the
pony's mouth with brandy from his flask, then
mounted and spurred on.

Another half-hour went by. He could see
that Pépe was in distress; his speed was by
degrees slacking. Would he last! Would he
last? Would the minutes that raced at his
side win in that hard race?

Houses again. Plastered fronts. All dark
and gray. No soul stirring. Sightless windows stared out upon emptiness. The plaza
bared its desolation to the pitiless moonlight.
Only from an unseen window a guitar hummed
and tinkled. All vanished. Open country
again. The solitude of the fields again; the
moonlight sleeping on the vast sweep of the
ranchos. Calpella past.

Felipe rose in his stirrups with a great shout.

At Calpella he knew he had crossed the divide.
The valley lay beneath him, and the moon was
turning to silver the winding courses of the
Rio Esparto, now in plain sight.

It was between Calpella and Proberta that
Pépe stumbled first. Felipe pulled him up and
ceased to urge him to his topmost speed. But
five hundred yards farther he stumbled again.
The spume-flakes he tossed from the bit were
bloody. His breath came in labouring gasps.

But by now Felipe could feel the rising
valley-mists; he could hear the piping of the
frogs in the marshes. The ground for miles had
sloped downward. He was not far from the
river, not far from Caliente, not far from the
Convent of Santa Teresa and Buelna.

But the way to Caliente was roundabout,
distant. If he should follow the road thither
he would lose a long half-hour. By going
directly across the country from where he now
was, avoiding Proberta, he could save much
distance and precious time. But in this case
Pépe, exhausted, stumbling, weak, would have
to swim the river. If he failed to do this
Felipe would probably drown. If he suc-
ceeded, Caliente and the convent would be
close at hand.

For a moment Felipe hesitated, then suddenly made up his mind. He wheeled Pépe

from the road, and calling upon his last remaining strength, struck off across the country.

The sound of the river at last came to his ears.

"Now, then, Pépe," he cried.

For the last time the little horse leaped to the sound of his voice. Still at a gallop, Felipe cut the cinches of the heavy saddle, shook his feet clear of the stirrups, and let it fall to the ground; his coat, belt and boots followed. Bareback, with but the headstall and bridle left upon the pony, he rode at the river.

Before he was ready for it Pépe's hoofs splashed on the banks. Then the water swirled about his fetlocks; then it wet Felipe's bare ankles. In another moment Felipe could tell by the pony's motion that his feet had left the ground and that he was swimming in the middle of the current.

He was carried down the stream more than one hundred yards. Once Pépe's leg became entangled in a sunken root. Freed from that, his hoofs caught in grasses and thick weeds. Felipe's knee was cut against a rock; but at length the pony touched ground. He rose out of the river trembling, gasping and dripping. Felipe put him at the steep bank. He took it bravely, scrambled his way—almost on his knees—to the top, then stumbled badly and fell prone upon the ground.

Felipe twisted from under him as he fell and
regained his feet unhurt.   He ran to the brave
little fellow's head.
"Up, up, my Pépe. Soh, soh."
Suddenly he paused, listening.   Across the
level fields there came to his ears the sound
of the bell of the convent of Santa Teresa tolling
for midnight.

.   .   .   .   .   .

Upon the first stroke of midnight the procession of nuns entered the nave of the church.
There were some thirty in the procession.
The first ranks swung censers; those in the rear
carried lighted candles.   The Mother Superior
and Buelna, the latter wearing a white veil,
walked together.   The youngest nun followed
these two, carrying upon her outspread palms
the black veil.
Arrived before the altar the procession
divided into halves, fifteen upon the east side
of the chancel, fifteen upon the west.   The
organ began to drone and murmur, the censers
swung and smoked, the candle-flames flared
and attracted the bats that lived among the
rafters overhead.   Buelna knelt before the
Mother Superior.   She was pale and a little
thin from fasting and the seclusion of the cells.
But, try as she would, she could not keep her
thoughts upon the solemn office in which

she was so important a figure. Other days
came back to her. A little girl gay and free
once more, she romped through the hallways
and kitchen of the old *hacienda* Martiarena
with her playmate, the young Felipe; a young
schoolgirl, she rode with him to the Mission
to the instruction of the *padre;* a young woman,
she danced with him at the *fête* of All Saints at
Monterey. Why had it not been possible that
her romance should run its appointed course to
a happy end? That last time she had seen him
how strangely he had deported himself. Untrue
to her! Felipe! Her Felipe; her more than
brother! How vividly she recalled the day.
They were returning from the Mission, where
she had prayed for his safe and speedy return.
Long before she had seen him she heard the
gallop of a horse's hoofs around the turn of the
road. Yes, she remembered that—the gallop
of a horse. Ah! how he rode—how vivid it
was in her fancy. Almost she heard the
rhythmic beat of the hoofs. They came nearer,
nearer. Fast, furiously fast hoof-beats. How
swift he rode. Gallop, gallop—nearer, on they
came. They were close by. They swept
swiftly nearer, nearer. What—what was this?
No fancy. Nearer, nearer. No fancy this.
Nearer, nearer. These—ah, Mother of God
—are real hoof-beats. They are coming;

they are at hand; they are at the door of the church; they are *here!*

She sprang up, facing around. The ceremony was interrupted. The frightened nuns were gathering about the Mother Superior. The organ ceased, and in the stillness that followed all could hear that furious gallop. On it came, up the hill, into the courtyard. Then a shout, hurried footsteps, the door swung in, and Felipe Arillaga, ragged, dripping, half fainting, hatless and stained with mud, sprang toward Buelna. Forgetting all else, she ran to meet him, and, clasped in each other's arms, they kissed one another upon the lips again and again.

The bells of Santa Teresa that Felipe had heard that night on the blanks of the Esparto rang for a wedding the next day.

Two days after they tolled as passing bells. A beautiful woman had been found drowned in a river not far from the house of Lopez Catala, on the high road to Monterey.

THE END